JAMES/FLINT/THRALL FAMILY LETTERS
SOUTHERN ILLINOIS 1870–1898

James/Flint/Thrall Family Letters

Southern Illinois 1870–1898

Edited by Harold A. Henderson, CG

Harold A. Henderson

2021

James/Flint/Thrall family letters, Southern Illinois, 1870–1898

2021, ed. Harold A. Henderson, CG, La Porte, Indiana

librarytraveler@gmail.com

Subjects: Genealogy, Family History, Correspondence, Letters, 19th Century, Illinois, Bone Gap, McKendree College, Methodism, Thrall, Flint, James

First Printing 2021

ISBN 978-1-7343-752-3-7

Printed in the United States

Table of Contents

Introduction

What would you give to spend a day with your great-grandparents? Or with a great-great grandmother?

We can't do that, but we do have perhaps the next best thing: 106 letters and fragments written by various members of the Flint and Thrall families of southern Illinois—most of them to or from Edith (Flint) Thrall and her husband Rev. Leonidas Thrall, their five children, and a few others, between 1870 and 1898. They begin with Leonidas and Edith's acquaintance and courtship at McKendree College in Lebanon, Illinois, and end with Edith's death there in 1898 at the age of 53.

The letters are both fascinating and difficult. They often take for granted daily things that we don't understand or have never dealt with (such as the almost constant necessity for sewing). Some are serious, some hopeful, some witty. One describes an impromptu small-town Fourth of July.

Asthma and its complications ran in the family. Almost every letter included information on who had sent whom a letter recently and on everyone's current state of health. Visits to "the doctor" sometimes included hair-raising diagnoses and prescriptions.

This collection is far from complete. We don't know exactly how these particular letters and fragments thereof managed to survive for more than a century. Frequent moves from parsonage to parsonage surely didn't help; it was Methodist church policy to move preachers every few years. Early in the 21st century various descendants started typing the handwritten and faded letters so that they could be read more easily and placed in their approximate order.

Probably the most significant savers and preservers were the first three generations: Leonidas and Edith themselves, their oldest child Edith Laura "Edie" Thrall, and Edie's niece Miriam (Thrall) Foster, who introduced younger family members to Edith Flint's letter on what we would now call feminism (letter 13). Writing to her future husband, she explained what she learned at the age of ten: that she had to give way to a brother, because she was only a girl. "For the first time in my life the idea suddenly dawned upon me that if it was not a crime to be born a girl it was at least a misfortune."

No one alive today knew Edith or heard her speak. The surviving letters may not be the ones she would have chosen to preserve, but they provide clues and glimpses of 19th-century lives—in some ways different from ours, and in other ways familiar.

Harold Henderson (librarytraveler@gmail.com) March 2021

Unless otherwise noted, the letters below were sent among Flint and Thrall family members and transcribed by Robin and Harold Henderson August 2000, January 2001, and March 2002, with later accessions, thanks to cousin Sally Simmons Thrall, and help from Lois Henderson. Most letters have been left as written, regardless of present-day spellings and usage.

WHO'S WHO IN THESE LETTERS?

William Flint (1816–1878) & Mary (Gedney) Flint (1815–1898) were the parents of eight children:

Mary A. (Flint) Nelson (1843–1898)

Edith Marie (Flint) Thrall (1845-1898) [EMF or EFT]

George W. Flint (1847–1926)

John Wesley Flint (1849–-1926)

James Gedney Flint (1850–1927)

Matthew Henry Flint (~1853–1924)

Samuel F. "Fletcher" Flint (1855–1923)

William Winterton Flint (1858–1896)

Worthy Thrall (1809–1852) & Hannah (James) Thrall (1809–1875) were the parents of four children who lived to grow up:

Mary Elizabeth (Thrall) Morgan (1833–1903)

Laura Lucina (Thrall) Gould (1835–1898)

Hannah Caroline (Thrall) Campbell (1845–1924)

Leonidas Worthy Thrall (1850–1918) [LWT]

Edith Marie (Flint) Thrall & Leonidas Worthy Thrall were the parents of:

Edith Laura Thrall (1874–1950)

Victor Worthy Thrall (1877–1963)

William Flint Thrall (1880–1941)

Charles Haven Thrall (1883–1968)

Harold Leonidas Thrall (1885–1966)

Many of the above individuals are profiled in more detail elsewhere: *Midwestern Methodists: Four Thrall Generations from Bone Gap, Illinois, 1809–2018* by Harold Henderson (2020), available for purchase at lulu.com or amazon.com.

This book is fully indexed by letter number, NOT by page number. A few selections:

EMF, letter 9, early 1870s: The trials you bade me look at *[as a minister's wife]* I have reviewed and now will set them in order before me just as they present themselves to me. A life of voluntary renunciation of all the vanities of riches when wealth is the end and aim of life for many. A way farer's tent and friends of brief acquaintance[,] ties made and broken until the heart's love for friends is scattered among hundreds instead of concentrated on few—all this when with many the associations that cling around one spot of earth, one round of familiar faces, seem the one thing dear next to life. All this—and this is all.

EFT, letter 19, 1879: On the Christmas tree Lonnie got a nice overcoat, a pair of socks and a chicken. I got eleven yards of good black cashmere with all the lining buttons and silk ready to make it up, a box of notions for the children, and from a milliner in town the children got two pair of stocking each, a pair of gloves each some pretty gingham dresses (which I shall not make up till spring). Vick received a box of blocks and Edie a picture book and a box of doll clothes with a dollie to wear them.

William W. Flint *[EFT's youngest brother]*, **letter 49, 1893:** Dr. Amick says I am a kind of curiosity—my right and left lung being as differently affected as though they belonged to two different persons. My right lung is asthmatic and my left is partially solidified, but says his treatment for asthma will cure both.

Charles Haven Thrall, letter 50 *[about age ten]*: There was two cisterns by the [parsonage] until this afternoon and then one of them caved in and the pump went down and the water is nearly to the top and it looks awful bad. Some men are coming tomorrow to fill it up.

EFT, letter 55, 1894: She *[cousin Mary Easterwood]* has been the patient nurse of her brother, mother, and two sisters all now dead, and for four years has been speaking low and stepping softly for fear of disturbing the sick one.

EFT, letter 72, 1896 *[to LWT at a Methodist gathering in Cleveland]*: It seems there are some men in the conference who grow excited over trifles. You know when a vessel is full it runs over, whether it holds a hogshead or a gill.

Annie (Kirkland) Flint on the farm near Raymond, Illinois, to sister-in-law EFT, letter 82, 1897: Of course there is plenty work to keep one busy and the season has been so late that we have little to show for all we have done—Friday George *[EFT's brother]* finished planting corn 40 acres—but of course that is all in the future. Last year he had the same when the floods came and destroyed almost half of it and greatly damaged the remainder. This year it may be the drouth. We know not.

EFT on the death of her sister-in-law Laura (Thrall) Gould, letter 88, 1898: After a long life of suffering bravely borne she rests. Her life of pain is not the most prominent thought that remains. Her great energy and the amount of work done by her would shame most of the healthy people by whom we are surrounded.

EFT, letter 96, 1898, to son William Flint Thrall: You are climbing one of lifes hills this summer, Willie. There are still higher ones before you but you will never climb another with the inexperience with which you set out last June. You may have lost some faith in humanity but you are now better able to value the world's promises at their real price or worth.

James/Flint/Thrall family letters 1870–1898

Written on back (by Harold L. Thrall?): "Letter of papa's mother to the folks in Bone Gap while she was in Lebanon and papa was in college. I think Wog is papa." The children Hannah refers to are Mary's children Milton, Allyn, Wilbur, and Maria Lucretia "Crete" Morgan. I have added punctuation and corrected spelling to make it more readable. RKH

1. HJT (Hannah James Thrall) in Lebanon to daughters (Mary Elizabeth Thrall Morgan) and (Laura Lucina Thrall Gould) in or near Bone Gap May 1870

May 1870 St Clare, Lebanon, Ill.

Dear Lizzie,

We were all glad to get a letter from you we are all well at present. Call and Wog are so busy I must answer your letter. They have some fine times in college and trust profitable. We still have good Tuesday evening prayer meetings. Lonny goes to every meeting of late.

If sinners will go to hell from Lebanon, I do not believe this praying band will have to answer for their sins any more than Noah, Elijah, or Daniel of old would have to answer for the sins of the unbelieving stubborn sinners in their time. When they are solemnly warned by precept and example having the eyes of their understanding inlighted and they see what is for their eternal good and refuse to yield to the gospels' plan for salvation they will be condemned but God's people will be clear of their guilt.

I must confess there are some cold professors [who] to all appearance go after the world and fashion and vanity more than after God. It costs ten dollars to get a dress made in the fashion so much trimming and flouncing. How vain it does look and how displeasing to Him who suffered so much to redeem a lost and ruined world from sin and death and to bring us back to happiness and favor with himself.

How is Milton doing, is he still serving Jesus as his best friend. I hope he is. I am glad Crete can write so well. Think she will make a good writer. I am so glad Allen can write, which hand does he write with? Tell Willie to write *[illegible]*. Why don't Milton ever write? I hope to see you all soon.

Who and when will it be convenient to meet us at the depot the 3 or 4 of June. Let us know, we will meet you at Olney Friday or Saturday noon. Write and let us know when it will suit the best. You better come with the big wagon for us, we want to bring our trunks and chest with us, what we put freight will not come to Olney the same day that we do and now Lizzie the worst of it, we have no dinner and in debt 13 dollars. We want you to send some soon. Tell Laura and Solon we will want forty dollars. If you can't get it no other way, get it off Mr. Bride. Send some right soon. Call and Wog say if they can get in to business here they will stay. I don't want them to stay. What do you think of it? Write soon and let me know. Your mother

[On other side of same paper:]

Dear Laura,

You said if we would stay through spring term you would see that we would have money to take us through. I guess you will find it *[illegible line]* tried to be saving. Lonny feels so bad about it but we all come out right if we do the best we can and leave the rest with God, that is all we can do. Do you know of any school Call could get? Write and let *[us]* know. Don't let anybody see this letter. Don't tell, only hurry. Thanks. Kiss the children for me. My love to Solon, yours truly, your mother.

(I leave all to you anytime).

2. LWT to EMF 6 February 1871

Compliments of L.W. Thrall to Miss Flint, asking the pleasure of her company next Wed. evening to the "Church Supper"

Lebanon, Ill.

Feb. 6th, 1871.

3. EMF in Lebanon to LWT 12 April 1871

Lebanon, Illinois

April 12, 1871

Dear Lonnie,

Although this letter must be written in great haste yet I think I cannot let tomorrow's mail go out without it. This morning's mail brought yours to me. Wesley's came yesterday. *[EMF's brother John Wesley Flint]* I must confess I was disappointed in the news from Carrie *[Hannah Caroline Thrall, older sister of LWT]*. I had so hoped to hear that she was much better. We cannot read the future—God knows that this is best for us.
Mary *[Flint, EMF's sister]* came home last Monday evening bringing Brother Nelson *[Rev. Horatio Nelson, later Mary's husband]* with her. He came to school for me last night and brought me up this morning so you see I have had two buggy-rides with a Methodist preacher this week.

I never told anyone a word of what you said to me until last Sunday evening. After we came home from church Wesley commenced a conversation which ended in my telling him the whole story. Imagine my astonishment when he quietly remarked, "I am not at all surprised." I asked "Why?" "I have but one reason to give" said he. "I knew it would come sooner or later. I have only one thing to say, consider the matter well; count the cost as well as the gain; think of him and his life-work, of yourself and your ability to sympathise with and assist him in it, of time and of eternity."

These thoughts, Lonnie, were not new to me. I have thought of all these. No man in the world needs a good wife as does a minister and with me the question is "Am I worthy? Can I be the counselor, comforter and friend that you need?" O, I think of it—think of it. The eyes of the world both religious and profane scan the minister's wife with a keener scrutiny if possible than that directed upon him. If he for any reason fails, many say, "It is her fault, what a pity so gifted a man had not made a more judicious choice."

Do not think, Lonnie, that I weakly shrink from this ordeal. I do not fear the world's scrutiny or criticisms if unjust; but in my case would they be wholly unjust? Would I not in some unguarded moment or at some unguarded point give occasion for offense?

I believe you are destined to do a great work in this grandest scene in life's drama and no hindering cause must exist. Perhaps you will think I am drawing a dark picture just to have you find the bright side for me. Not so. These considerations must be taken into account and that too, now. A time might come when it would be too late. I see nothing but is right in your plan for the future in regard to study. Only one thing I have to say—take time enough. Do not hurry yourself or work too hard. We will have an opportunity to talk it over before long, if we conclude to take it together.

I have some thought of going to St. Louis or Mt. Vernon next winter. Don't mention this to anyone but tell me what you think of it. If I go to St. Louis it will be to write not to teach, for some things I think I should like it better. All things are pleasant here, rather pleasanter than usual indeed. A lady lectures here tonight or rather she will read. I do not like her subject and will hardly attend.

I am glad you are so pleasantly situated. How do you like trigonometry? I was rather well pleased with it after I fairly understood enough to go ahead. Wesley and I have some times over Cicero.

Y.H. McBride has been near death with typhoid pneumonia. He is out of danger, but his brother W.E. went home to see him and is now very sick with the same disease.

S.P. Spark was at church last Sunday evening with his wife. She was his choice, but I don't fancy her very much myself. But I do wrong to judge with so little knowledge.

I did not tell you quite all Wesley said in regard to you and me. Perhaps I would better not just now. The next morning he met me in the hall and said he had some more to say to me on the subject. I will tell you all sometime I think.

When you see Carrie again tell her that her friends here have not forgotten her. It is a constant inquiry, "What is the last news from Carrie?"

I thank you for your good letter. So far as I am concerned you would have been welcome to read the letter I wrote Carrie. Perhaps I will tell you something when I write again.

I am   Edith

4. LWT in Bone Gap to EMF (first 4 pages only) 16 April 1871

Bone Gap Ill April 16th 1871

Dear Edith:

I returned from Olney last Friday evening about ten oclock and found your letter lying on the table for me. The hour being late and I somewhat weary with a drive of fifty five miles over rough roads, I did not prepare an answer to send to Albion next morning as I otherwise would have done. Our Bone Gap semiweekly mail is so slow that I can not endure to be governed by it when it can be avoided in writing to you. I am now working on the farm and will perhaps be *obliged* to use this slow routine for a short time. But what a long introduction I am writing!

I saw Carrie *[probably LWT's older sister Hannah Caroline Thrall]* Friday. She is stronger, has a better appetite, feels less pain and, to outward appearances, is better. But I asked the Dr. what he thought were the chances for a *permanent* cure and he answered "They are not very flattering." *[Editor's note: Carrie outlived all her siblings.]* Dr. Scudder of Cincinnati has prescribed another remedy in addition to the treatment which she is already receiving and which he (Scudder) thinks will likely remove the main difficulty. What effect it has will be apparent by the date of my next letter. She was much pleased by the reception of your letter and will write as soon as she can do so safely even if it be but little.

Your conversation with Wes *[EFT's younger brother John Wesley Flint]* and his being "not at all surprised" remind me of something which I must mention. I thought I knew that the idea had found way into his brain, from the following circumstance. I think it was the Sunday evening following the church Festival, when I went out to your house with Jim from Sabbath School. You will remember that we went to church that evening in a sleigh. To me it was an exceedingly pleasant

11

ride and, as I sat in the church that night, the sentiment which had been for some time struggling for dominion in my heart with constantly increasing aggressiveness seemed to have reached a climax, although it had so far met with a manful resistance; —a resistance, feeble, not the less, however, since it was conscious of having nothing tangible to support it—and for the first time I half-determined upon an important measure; — half yielded to that which was plainly enough the dictates of both feelings and judgment. Perhaps *[illegible]*, though I would not then have acknowledged it. (It was just previous to this that I had written on the subject to Carrie.)

Wesley and I were sitting together and when the sermon was about half finished he spoke to me with regard to something which the speaker had remarked and I was astonished to discover that I had not heard a word of the sermon and knew nothing of the text or subject. During the evening I wrote to him on a slip of paper a sentence very foreign to the subject upon which I was thinking and before *[illegible line]* pretended to say something in answer to it and made a remark which at once convinced me that he had guessed the thoughts which were really on my mind. Whatever it was, the sentence has gone for me now; but I remember distinctly that *[illegible line]* thought him very sound in *[illegible]* idea which lay behind and prompted it. (What I had written to him was with regards to going to Evanston.) After I had got to the foot of *[remainder is lost]*

5. EMF to LWT 11 March 1872

Compliments of E. M. Flint to Mr. L.W. Thrall, and accepts his invitation for this evening.

At Home Monday 5 P.M.

March 11./72

Excuse my pencil, if you please

6. EMF to LWT 19 March 1872/1873

At Home, Tues. eve Mar. 19.

Dear Lonnie,

Have just returned from Trenton, where I have spent the day. Have
called on several old schoolmates and enjoyed the day much. I guess I
will go there and open a class soon. I dont know how well it will pay,
but pretty well after we are well started, I do not doubt. My class will
contain ages "very various" and both ladies and gentlemen. I received a
letter from New Douglass *[Madison County]*. I can go there if I wish, but
after considering all things have concluded that I would better go to
Trenton.

I wish very much to make myself as perfect as possible in drawing and
painting, and will have little or no opportunity to do anything at it up
there. I thank you earnestly for your scrap, always pay attention to
anything on that subject, but with the author agree that fruit and flowers
are not the highest type of painting and would add that no
representation of nature (however charming to the eye) can live long
unless it embody some idea, thus appealing to a higher faculty than the
mere love of beauty.

My "Yosemite Valley" will be finished tomorrow and I expect to take it
to Mrs. Sheperd Saturday or Monday. Do you want to see it? I very
much wish you to see it by daylight if at all. When do you mean to come
out? You said if I wanted to see you before you came to write and that
led me to suppose you had some time set in your own mind. *I am always
glad to see you,* but never wish you to break upon any duty to visit me, so
come whenever you can and you will find me at home and a hearty
welcome *for you.*

Mary met Bro. Clins *[?]* and heard all about your meeting at Lake
Branch. I remembered your request more especially in the afternoon
and at night. I staid at home at night. They held a meeting last night but
I dont know whether there is meeting tonight or not. Bro C. thinks the
prospect good, which is no poor compliment to you.

Lonnie, do I do you good or not by telling such things? I would not
flatter you for worlds, but I do like you to know that I appreciate you
and am pleased when others do so, too. I told you once that I never

would mention you *[illegible]* unless she first spoke of you first—and by name too. Well I kept my word and last Saturday evening she did speak to me of you. But she did not say anything about you that I could not listen to with pleasure. I cant write it all. She wished something for herself that I thought might be true for *me*. Are you going to the wedding tomorrow night. I think I shall. I hope your cough is quite well or at least much better. I am very tired tonight.

Edith

7. EMF to LWT, undated fragment

come by way of Olney or shall you come by Southern road? You want to go to Belleville before Sunday preceding conference. I have often wondered whether it would not be possible for you to make that your landing place and let some one from here meet you there. In that case you would not need to go down there again. We are looking for Wesley *[EMF's brother]* early next week. He says he is tired of begging—collecting. This reminds me of one of the preachers at Dist. Conf. He said he had marked down all he had taken and occasionally he took out his discipline and counted over those still remaining. Had not yet got through but would endeavor to do so if there were enough Sundays left before conference. What are you taking the collections for Bro E. asked the P.E. *[presiding elder]*. Some of them for conscience sake and others because the discipline so requires. Well I don't profess to know anything about them.

We have heard from George *[younger brother George W. Flint]* several times, mostly by postal cards, once we received a long and very interesting letter dated Burlington *[Iowa]* Aug 13. Our latest was the 15th Red Oak Junction Iowa. He seems very much pleased with the country thus far. James *[younger brother James G. Flint]* says he is going out there next summer while Henry *[younger brother Matthew Henry Flint]* is as determined on seeing Colorado sooner or later.

James has determined not to go to college this fall. Says he is going to dismiss the tenant from the old farm and take charge of both places. This is quite an undertaking. His health is not very firm and I am afraid the care of over three hundred acres of farmed land will break him down, but he says that make money he must and will during the next year and a half.

I know it is necessary for some one take charge. Pa's health *[father William Flint]* has been very poor this summer. At first the three younger boys held back; but then they gave up at last and are as deeply interested as any one now in plans for the coming year. Wesley and Fletcher will enter college.

Well darling are you tired of my long talk on this subject. You begged pardon for talking about yourself. I beg pardon for this.

Something singular must have prompted your dream last Sunday night. I do not think I had more than an hour's good sound sleep that night, not because I was sick myself but on account of a sick roommate. Poor Nellie! Of course I thought of you and presently traced out your picture on the wall, as it hung there in its frame. It is most time for me to go to something else and darling I will bid you good night for a little while. If I have forgotten anything forgive me. I will tell you all when I see you and that is only about five weeks now. Dear love may God be with you

Edith.

8. EMF to LWT, undated fragment, page 9

heart of so strong a worker. I feel ready to suffer and to do if [it] so be that God will employ me.

Another reason for wishing to assist you is my own improvement. I cannot keep up with you in your methods of thought or your knowledge of things both temporal and spiritual unless I study and think and constantly keep some mental work in hand. I can never bear the thought of being so far behind you in mental progress that I shall be unable to follow your reasoning and prove your conclusions. I would understand what interests *you*. To do this I must not be a mere hearer of your words, I must do something myself.

Tell me darling what you think of my arguments. I am anxious to know. I am covering much paper whether with many words or not. A very gloomy look *[lines illegible]* large class and expects to make up a hundred dollars. Prof. Swahlen was married yesterday. Now darling goodbye you know that if you were here you would receive what you dreamed of in addition to my words goodbye. May God be with you love always. Your own Edith

9. EMF to LWT, undated, last 4 pages, undated *[dream sequence]*

is a mystery connected with it. I have a presentiment that there is some one in it that you know. I went. Some one at the door gave me the names of the occupants, strange names to me. Entering the room a gentleman met me saying "You are just the person I wished to see. My poor friend I think is dying." I approached the man and there dusty and travel worn, old and rapidly sinking into death's arms lay he whom I had known as Marvin. I called him several times and presently he knew me and began to ask forgiveness for the past. I hushed him—told him death was near and he must think of other things. Just then the door opened and some one called me twice. I looked and it was you. You called again— "Edith, I want you." I turned away from the dying man and went out to you. That was all. There is no significance, save as you may read it. *You have conquered.* I would not have had it end otherwise.

Again comes back the old vexed question of promises. They are the offspring of weak faith. If I could not trust you Lonnie without promises of fidelity I would fear to trust you at all. If I trust you wholly I require no promises save your presence. I want to see you and take an outlook. Settle at once and forever our question. I do not wish to wrong you. I think of all a life with you implies.

The trials you bade me look at I have reviewed and now will set them in order before me just as they present themselves to me. A life of voluntary renunciation of all the vanities of riches when wealth is the end and aim of life for many. A way farer's tent and friends of brief acquaintance[,] ties made and broken until the heart's love for friends is scattered among hundreds instead of concentrated on few— all this when with many the associations that cling around one spot of earth, one round of familiar faces, seem the one thing dear next to life. All this—and this is all. I am strong enough to trust in Jehovah's strength and that is all he asks.

You paint a beautiful picture of a coming life. It *[is]* all I could wish for, that the one best able should aid the other over the weary places in the journey. I think I never could love a man who did *[not?]* hold the issues of eternity in more estimation than this little life. I want to talk the matter over with you again. Do you know I often look back to that evening we spent together and wish that it was to come over again. There are so many things I should have said that were hushed on my lips, while some were said that would as well have been left unsaid. I wonder if it will be always thus.

I remember *[illegible]* day when you came down to the school house. Well here I am nearing the bottom of the eighth page and have only written on subjects that directly concern myself. Have I made the dark places clear to you? Do you understand me any better now, and are you satisfied with my explanations? When do you expect to be in Lebanon? *[illegible]* hurry for anything I have said. Come just when it will be most to your interest. I will be more pleased than I can readily tell when I receive another letter from Carrie. Tell her I am so glad to hear she is better. It seemed a long time until your letter came this week. It will not be so long next time, I guess.

Edith

10. EMF to LWT 17 July 1873

Pleasant Valley Ills.

Jan 17. 1873

My Darling

Friday morning finds with no letter written for you and a prospect of only a very poor one for this week. I have been a little sick again. Not sick either but worried and tired when night comes. The weather has been very disagreeable sometimes rainy and today extremely cold again. Aint I a complainer Lonnie? A sad story has just been told me, about midnight last night a lady in the neighborhood died. Her husband is a man in very moderate circumstances and there are left five little girls, one not quite two years old. Already they are talking of separating them and wondering who will take this one and that one.
I have thought of you at your meeting almost constantly this week. Lonnie Dearest[,] God is answering my earnest prayer and making my darling a firebrand in the world. That your call is a true call from God

has been demonstrated by the conversion of so many souls through your instrumentality. May He ever continue his loving kindness and every day fill your heart with the deepest and most lasting joy. I pray for this constantly. I think I shall much enjoy next winter with you and anticipate much spiritual advancement. With you I always grow better. Would God that I could be as useful to you as you already *[have]* been to me.

When coming out from your meetings these bitter cold nights please be very careful of yourself. Remember that there is much yet for you to do and think too how much pain it will give me to know that you *[illegible]* while doing your holy work. Have you settled on your home yet? and how is your mother? I am very anxious to hear from her. Do you know why Carrie does not write to me any more? It has been *so* long since I heard from her. I know she is very busy but I would like to hear from her if it was only a line or two. As my letter is so uninteresting this time I will send you a part of a letter from Wesley. The first sheet was full of an account of a sick spell he has had and the beginning of the account of his first funeral.

I was informed Wednesday night that my father was buried last Monday. I knew the report was utterly false for he brought me out to my school Sunday evening in usual health. I cannot imagine what can have started such a report. The small pox is very bad in Trenton and has almost broken up school and church too. It has *[illegible]* made its appearance in Lebanon. I do not fear it.

Last night I was dreaming of you all night. Have scarcely failed to dream of you every night this week and am very anxious to get home and get your letter. I try sometimes to imagine how it would seem to go home on Friday night and not find your letter there awaiting me.

Clara *[not identified]* came out with me this week and seems to be very well acquainted with the children. Dear love remember always that I love you as I love none other and as none other can love you darling and that as the days go by this deep and trusting love is daily increasing. Pray for me darling Lonnie for I need your prayer very much. With deepest love, Edith

11. EMT to LWT 25 February 1873

Pleasant Valley.

Feb. 25. 1873

Dear Heart,

Your three good letters came during last week. I was delighted with so much good in a single week. This is your "rest week" and I am glad that after so long a term of hard work you have an opportunity to rest a little. Do some resting for me, won't you Lonnie!

Wednesday, well here I am once more darling. I only wrote a few words last night and then it was *[illegible]* winter. Never found a winter so long before. And sometimes I think of winters to come that will not be long enough. Only seven months! Well it can't be much longer than that. I am anxious for our bishops to finish their plan of the conferences. Every time I open the Central I look for its completion and have grown weary of reading the old one over.

I shall be thinking of you all through the session of your quarterly meeting. May God be with you and aid you in your working. I am so very glad Bro. Massey will be there. Wesley is to be alone this time. I am in very good health at present and hope to remain so. I think my chief trouble was from that blow on my head and I dont feel anything more of it now. Two weeks from next Friday my school will close. The school is very full now. I have averaged this far during this month thirty-four per day. They think the school is very large.

S.H. Parkinson was teaching and preaching somewhere not far from home and he got into difficulty with the sons of the directors and was told that if he could not agree with them they had no use for him and he might consider himself dismissed, which he did. Don't you think there is a brilliant prospect for the next teacher in that school?

Darling I love you deeply and constantly. I can think of but little else. Often it happens when writing to you that a great silence seems to fall upon my heart and I ask not for words to say only for my dear one's quiet restful presence. You remember in our past experience that many an hour has passed when we have said but few words and trusted to the silent eloquence of loving hearts to tell dear old story. Just as I feel this afternoon and I think *[if]* only I could know that the end of the day's work would bring you to me I would care little for the toil. Dear heart our lives will be like a dream and your sweet picture of a fairy land will in reality be ours some one of these happy days.

[change of ink]

Suddenly interrupted by the arrival of Mary and Wesley I have brought my letter here to finish for I have just found out that I shall not be at home till a week from Y day *[?]* and so to save my darling from a disappointment I will send him a poor little letter. I hope to hear from you next Friday but it is by no means certain.

Darling will we ever tell each other all that the heart of each holds for each other? I am waiting so very impatiently for your next visit. Some way I am not easily taught to do without you. Well dear I dont want to learn the lesson, but it makes me a little lonely when my soul's best life is away. When I write again I will tell you more news from Wes. He too expects to commence a meeting after his quarterly meeting *[;]* it is a week later than I told you. He wishes to be remembered and would be very glad to hear from you. He says he knows how to sympathize with your winter work.

Pray for me Lonnie darling and know that you are dearest of all earth to me and ever in my mind. Lovingly Edith

[written sideways on front page]

I send you Wesley picture to keep it from other hands. Take care of it for me love will you not?

You understand why I address you with blue ink and write the better part of the letter with black ink. They are making a great fuss around talking of measuring Wesley's back to see how wide it is. He has got exceedingly *fat*. Well dear Lonnie we are having a happy evening. O darling if you were here I should be almost too happy to exist. Soon we will know how very dear and happy we can make life to each other.

Edith

12. EMF to LWT 9 April 1873

Pleasant Valley Lebanon Ills.

April 9. 1873

Dearest *[Lonnie?]*

Again I take my seat at the old pulpit and wonder just what you think of me as you read the date of this letter. Sometime ago I wrote a letter and imagined it would be the last one I should ever write to you from this place and now I have a prospect of writing at least seven more from the old pulpit. I have changed its place and now I turn my face toward your country whenever I sit down. Perhaps you would laugh to have seen me using the pen I am now writing with for a spoon to eat my dinner with a few minutes ago. I can as you see adapt myself to any given set of circumstances always*[,]* requiring however either your presence or the hope that soon it will be mine.

Dear love school goes on very well thus far. I asked for twenty five scholars and they have given me the promise of more. Have only taught three days (and this is Thursday night) for Tuesday the rain fell incessantly that I did not think it wise to attempt to teach, had twenty eight scholars yesterday and today. Oh I know the time will soon pass and I hope to clear thirty five dollars at least and that may be useful sometime. I only undertook to teach forty days and shall close my school, if nothing happens, on the thirtieth of May, just a year from the day that I closed my drawing class last spring.
I dont think I shall try to finish this letter before I go home for I want to see your letter first. I expect it is at home ready for me and I shall go after it tomorrow evening. Shall have read it before twenty four more hours are past.

Do you ever think darling that I am odd in thus counting the hours that are to elapse before I shall read your precious letters? I used in the long ago *[to]* count the hours to pass before I should see the light of the dearest eyes the world to me and now that those glances are denied me for the present I transfer that thought to the dear words once mirrored in their gaze. I desire so much to make you happy that sometimes I question if the matter does not occupy nearly all my moments. Of course other thoughts *[illegible]* duties claim attention still away down in my hearts deepest recesses the picture exists and constantly I am *[illegible]* to soften it*[s]* tints, to add a gentler glory to its lights and a richer mellower tinge to its restful shadows. I can almost touch with hand of flesh its intangible beauty and in the still hours of the night I gaze on its growing loveliness until I can almost *[illegible]* hear the music of harmony, for to me a perfect-tone of music exists in harmonious shapes and delicate tints, while in the bolder strokes of stronger hands I hear the tumbling undertones of deeper sounds. How grand a picture we can make of our lives, my darling, how perfect a chord! All of my love is wound into your very being; *dearest of all created souls!* and I wait as now with tumbling and love freighted heart for that holiest of all hours when we shall covenant before both God and the world to be no more twain but one heart. Can you imagine of the existence of others who love with an affection as deep and strong as ours? Darling I ask for no other glory than a precedence in loving. It is to me a Godlike attribute.

Friday eve.

Darling I have today received your letter, hope for another tomorrow. May God bless you. Pray for me much dearest love, I need your prayers so much. I am not going home tonight. Jim *[brother]* is here and will take this letter to Lebanon. I want to tell you a long sad story when I write again. Again I ask pray for me constantly darling.

Edith

13. EMF to LWT 10 July 1873

Lebanon, Illinois

July 10, 1873

My Love

I am wanting to write you a very long letter but am again limited in my time. I write a day earlier than usual for I do not wish to disappoint you and if the morning is fine I expect to go to Belleville tomorrow to do some trading. Shall buy some housekeeping things for you and me next fall—in case we get married (but Bro. Kershey doesn't see a niche of time for a wedding). I am going to get some table cloths and towels and then in case you have to get to preaching I shall be able to help you a little in starting out.

Will you forgive me, Lonnie, if I differ from you once in a while? Some way I feel anxious to know just what are your thoughts on the subject. We cannot expect to live together through a long life without ever differing and in fact I am not particularly anxious to do so, if such a course would necessitate the forced yielding of well established opinions on the part of either one.

I was particularly pleased with your last letter. For some reason I had of late imagined that you differed from me very materially in regard to the matter you spoke of then. I am most agreeably disappointed. Cannot tell whence I gained the idea.

I do not remember what I wrote to Carrie last time on the suffrage question. Probably it was a very brief and not very carefully considered statement of my views. *I am not ultra,* but on the question of social and legal equality between man and woman I am radical and have been since my tenth year *[about 1855].* At that time a scene was enacted in which I as an actor was made to take the place McChamberlain spoke of when he said the sister was compelled to give in to her brother because he was a boy and she only a girl. For the first time in my life the idea suddenly dawned upon me that if it was not a crime to be born a girl it was at least a misfortune.

I do not imagine that the ballot is a panacea for all of wrongs or of evils. How can I when I see those who enjoy the privilege often wronged and cruelly oppressed. At present it may be that the ballot does not need the women but, Lonnie dear, *they* need the *ballot.*

Of late I have thought but little on the subject. Like yourself I consider the matter fated to succeed and I also agree with you in thinking that in God's good time it will be settled and that in the best way. As for Miss Anthony, well, we need a "John Brown" perhaps and I guess the country can spare her as well as any other unless it be Woodhull/Claflin. I am not at all astonished at her action, rather wonder that some one had not trodden the path before her but have no desire to have done so myself.

Should I ever be entrusted with so great a responsibility as a voice in our country's government I shall try to discharge my duty well and enjoy it as I do other privileges now granted to women that were but a short time ago denied them, for instance education and financial equality in wages paid for the same work done.

Do I pain you or grieve you, darling, by what I have said? Did you dream of me as different? I do so wish to make you happy that I am tempted sometimes to say that I would sooner yield any and every opinion rather than give you grief. Rather think that I should anyway if I could first be convinced both by argument and example that by so doing I could promote your happiness. You have set me to thinking on the matter and all night long last night I thought and dreamed of it and you together, and this morning I awoke as from a strange weird world to find it daylight and just above me on the wall your picture seemed to look on me with a questioning glance. As if you had wondered at my restless night, and was only waiting for me to wake and tell you the reason.

Well, Lonnie, you know I love you and I am just as certain that you love me and we will have no reason to fear for our future happiness if God will let us meet again.

Well, darling, just as I had written thus far, Clara came in from the office and brought me—not a letter—but something more precious than a letter from any one save yourself could be. A reminder of your loving care and thought of me in the shape of the July number of the Ladies Repository. I thank you so much the dear one who loves me and so gracefully expresses it. I shall read it with much pleasure. I am anxious to hear from Carrie again. I hope you will have a good chance to study now and not have to go to hard work again.

Wesley gave us a pleasant surprise by calling and staying over Monday night. We had no rain that morning but at four in the afternoon a fearful storm lasting for near two hours came on. No harm done however. Next Monday I will think of you as writing to me and now I must leave for a little while.

May God bless and ever protect my darling.

Lovingly

Edith

14. LWT to EMF, 1873?

Olney Tuesday morning

It is a little while before lunch time and Olney presenting nothing new at least at this time of the day I write you a word. I arrived here at ten last night and enjoyed a good night's rest. I will not say that I did not need it as yesterday morning found me somewhat tired.

Whisky was "all the go" on the train last night. The train was loaded with Dutchmen returning from the Singerfest. Nearly everyone in my car had a bottle which he occasionally drew, sipped, and handed to his neighbor. When my turn would come I had "thanks" for them. I will not touch it, for I see hell in it.

An old lady sat near me who, when the train stopped for supper, unrolled from a paper a piece of bread which the remains of her teeth were just sufficient to enable her to masticate. God bless her came involuntarily to my lips.

While I have been writing the above in the store here a drunken man assaulted me and cursing me of being a Catholic Joe. He said he "knew 'em by kind of insight." I paid little attention to him and at last he has left me.

I shall soon see my home but when evening comes shall not be surprised to find myself lonely. Home is no less dear to me than ever but the attraction far more powerful that I have left behind me will live in my thoughts nor will I seek to expel it. The rising tear may come, I will wipe it away and bid my soul rejoice what I have although it is distant and what will be with me again for life when a few months have unrolled. I have no more time. I will write you more on Friday and try to write it so you will not have so much difficulty in reading it as you will have in deciphering these scribbles. Love, L.

15. *[Undated notes between Leonidas and Edith some time between their engagement and their marriage]*

Tonight dear one? Yes, if ever.

Its the other side of the question that trembles I fear. Let me know just how you feel and what you think I feel like. Talk freely on any subject that may be on your mind tonight. Ah, there are a thousand things that may trouble your heart! There are ten thousand that may be this or that to each of us according to the standpoint from which each views them. Shall there not be perfect confidence between us now if there never has been? We are just as much one in God's sight as when our hands shall be joined by the minister at the marriage altar except the customs of society which are to be conscientiously regarded.

Can we not tell each other what we think, that is what I mean.

Dear Lonnie, will you forgive all that I have done wrong during the past nine months? I have done wrong to you oftener than you will now remember.

Wrong to me? Dear Edith, you never have—at least, if so I am very ignorant of the time, place or surroundings. Why do you think of such a thing?

I do not know hardly, only I have thought of it so much of late.

Tell me what you were thinking of. Tell me exactly Edith. I want to know the exact fact which I know you will tell me if you tell me anything. Will you not, Edith?

I will try. I *will* tell you as near as words can tell it and your knowledge of me will intuitively tell the unspoken thoughts.

16. EMF to LWT 21 August 1873

In my own room

Aug 21. 1873.

Dearest

How dear the privilege when seperated from you to be able to find so ready a servant as the letter. You say that words but feebly express thoughts when written. Spoken words are better yet even they sometimes sink into silence in the presence of nature's more eloquent voices. You have known such hours dear and I have known them too. In the future, now almost the present, we have promise of many such hours. May God grant that we may ever be as able to create and enjoy these seasons as at present! I know you to be noble true and most worthy. I respected you first and then on this foundation built a love for you and for you alone, a love so deeply implanted in my nature that naught can erase it or you from my soul.

You speak of your ignorance of woman's nature. Darling your own nature taught you how to strike with wonder-power *[?]* the most harmonious chords in my heart. Whether my own soul is an anomaly among women or not I will not attempt to decide, but this I can say—your full and warmhearted expressions of love suit me better than ought else I can imagine. I love you, and to love you perfectly I must know all I can find out about you. Else how can I tell when I best please him whom I so dearly love? You are frank, outspoken and loving in word deed and glance. How then could I doubt the purity and sweetness of a fountain sending forth such delightful waters? Darling I love you better and still better as you unveil to me your soul. You please me by telling all your thoughts as you now do. For worlds I would not have you draw between our souls a single fold of the vail [veil] of policy or cold conventionalism. I love you for what you are. Never be too proud my darling to tell me how well you love me. If you knew how dearly I prize every expression of your love there would be no question in your mind so far as we two are concerned about the freedom in expressing love.

Do you enjoy my letters when they talk of the love I bear you? Think of me darling as equally appreciative and you will always have at your command a treasure far dearer to me than wealth or fame.

Will not your contemplated meetings prevent you from being at home during your last Sunday before coming here? Do you intend to

[page(s) missing; written crossways on first page of letter]

I shall anxiously your next letter. Dont over work yourself this warm weather, I shall pray for you at your meetings. Have you said any thing to your folks about our wedding. I mean in regard to coming? I think of you pray for you and love you more than I can either write or tell in less than a lifetime. Your Edith

[Leonidas Worthy Thrall and Edith Marie Flint were married 29 September 1873]

17. LWT to HJT 7 July 1874

[note on envelope: Papa's letter to his mother one week after I was born. E. L. T.]

[addressed, Mrs. Hannah Thrall, Bone Gap, Edwards Co., Ill.]

July 7th 1874

Freeburg St. Clair Co. Ill.

Dear Mother & Sister

I have been a little negligent in answering your last letter but I presume you heard from me as I wrote to Laura not long ago. We are having some very warm weather now. The thermometer stands above 105 in the shade every day.

Last Monday week I went up to Lebanon and Miss Hattie Lord *[likely Edith's first cousin, acting as midwife]*—Edith's cousin—came back with me and is here now. The next Wednesday—July 1st—was a day of rejoicing in our little household. Of course the little cherub *[Edith Laura Thrall]* is pretty and from her mouth upwards—including her ears—she resembles Carrie more nearly than any other of her relations. Her eyes are blue; her mouth is Edith's exactly. She is twenty two inches long and has been generally reckoned to weigh about nine pounds though she has not been weighed and I think the estimate named a little high but not much. She is quiet and seems to feel quite well.

Edith thinks she favors our side of the house but I do not see very much difference if any myself. Edith is doing quite well except that she does not eat any. Sits up some, feels able to sit up more but is trying to be careful of overexercise. Today she is complaining of headache—something unusual with her—and does not feel quite as strong as she did yesterday. Mrs. Beetler [?] is her attendant and has endeared herself very to Edith by her tender care and faithfulness. Her house joins ours and she comes and dresses the baby every day and as soon as everything is attended to she is off again like a shot with a cheerful "alle recht Gute Morgen" always leaving encouragement and good hope behind her.

She is a German woman and can not speak a word of English so you may imagine we have interesting conversation. If our little visitor does not turn out to be a Dutchman it will not be because it lacked early Dutch training. Our Quarterly Meeting—the last for the year—will take place one week from next Saturday. District Conference at Sparta comes the Tuesday following.

Friday Afternoon. I intended to write a long letter this time but have been very busy since commencing this letter and you will have to excuse me. Tell Laura that I have beaten Professor Swahlen [?] by *at least six* pounds. She seemed very much interested in the matter not long ago. I see an announcement that there is a change of time in the holding of the Annual Conference from Sep 30 to 23. This will enable me to see you one week earlier than I had expected. How will we have to come?

It is going to be a very heavy expense to come to Albion by way of Carmi and Mt Carmel especially if we have to stay over night at both of those places. I guess we will come to your house as early in the week before Conf. meet as possible—that is about Sep 15. We will take the train at Lebanon if we come to Olney and the fare will be $3.75 apiece. If we come to Grayville we will have to take the train at [illegible] and come on the South eastern to Grayville by way of Carmi and the fare will be $5.25 apiece. So you can save us $3.00 more by meeting us at Olney than at Grayville and probably hotel bill over night at Carmi besides. It is going to cost a good deal any way we fix it. Edith sends love. Lonnie sends love.

18. EFT to sister Mary Flint 20 December 1878

Columbus, Kan.

Dec. 20, 1878.

Dear Mary

Your letter has been at hand for several days. I have all the while thought I would soon write but my days are full and often all my evenings too. We are all well. Lonnie has improved a great deal during the last two or three weeks. I really was alarmed for quite a while for he seemed to have no vital energy to enable him to strengthen. I am doing very well.

We manage to do our own work except the washing and ironing. I guess you laugh at my saying "we." Well I can assure you Lonnie does a great deal. When we get up he makes a fire and then gets breakfast while I dress the children and get them washed and ready for breakfast. We usually make coffee and fry meat and I keep light bread on hand. This makes a very comfortable breakfast. Then while I wash the dishes he makes a fire in the sitting room and sweeps the floor. Then we have prayers and I set the bedroom in order, while he goes to his studies till two oclock when he goes out to visit the people. Now you see how we manage to do without a girl. Our washing is done away from home and by a first-class laundress.

Bertha I suppose is in Iowa. She left here the 2nd of this month. I have a letter from Henry *[probably younger brother Matthew Henry]* today saying that he has not heard from her since the 19 of Nov. Mary I wish I knew that he would never hear from her again. Maybe he would feel bad for a while but I really think it would be the best thing for him. If I could see you I could tell you many things that would make you be of my opinion.

I am getting along very well with my sewing. Expect to cut some carpet rags next week. Well how is that boy prospering? Have you found a name for him yet Give my love to Etta and tell her I claim to be her Aunt. What is your latest news from Emma? *[these people not identified]* I have heard nothing at all since I saw you. We have had a thick sleet all over everything for a week and all day today it has tried to snow but has not made a very great success of it.

I think we will have a protracted meeting begin next Sunday. All things work very well and a deep feeling seems to pervade the church in general. The people are anxious to begin and seem to be ready to help in the work indeed are now helping all they can. The prayer meeting and class meetings are very interesting. We really have some of the best folks here I ever knew. This town does not allow a saloon but the whiskey element tried to get the upper hand with the ruse of drug stores and this town of one thousand inhabitants supports at present seven drug stores.

A few weeks ago a new city marshall was appointed. He is a Methodist and as soon as he took his office he began to walk the streets with his baton and watch everything. This week he began his work and has arrested every druggist in town with one or two exceptions and one person has been fined $1000.00 [?] dollars and the case of others are now coming on. He says he will clear the town of such a set and make room for a decent drug store, one that is fit for his wife or any other woman to step into. This at present is not the case. I say God speed Charlie McReynolds and every other man who tries [to] blot out drunkenness from our town and country.

I feel so sorry for Emma poor girl. Henry says Neely [?] is about the same. Some times he will be in bed till ten oclock and then go to bed again at four in the afternoon. Please write to me very soon. You have a better chance than I have and more leisure. Tell Mr. Nelson to write now and then. He used to write to me long ago. Mother has been real sick but is now better. How are [you?] going to spend christmas. Lonnie sends love.

Edith F. Thrall.

19. EFT to sister Mary Flint Nelson in Farmington, Missouri, 1 January 1880

Ashley, Ill. Jan. 1 1880

Dear Mary

I must not wait any longer to write to you. I was real glad to hear that you were enjoying yourselves so well. I hope your face did not get bad.

We are all well. The children are entirely over the whooping cough. They had it very light. I believe you saw them at their worst. Victor could hardly be fatter than when you saw him, but he is just as fat as then. Edie has gained considerable flesh and color. She is never as rosy as Victor but I believe her health is perfect now. Lonnie has suffered some from headache lately. I am well and have gained both in weight and strength since coming to Ashley.

We are very much pleased with the place and have good reason to be so. We have received over a hundred and fifty dollars on salary and about a hundred dollars in other ways. First a fifty dollar donation. Then one morning nearly a month ago we found a large hair arm chair standing on the porch. Col. Monroe who is not a church member but a real good old man came after a while and owned to bringing it. Now said he this is not quarterage, I shall pay that in money, but it is a token of friendship from myself and wife. Was not that good?

On the Christmas tree Lonnie got a nice overcoat, a pair of socks and a chicken. I got eleven yards of good black cashmere with all the lining buttons and silk ready to make it up, a box of notions for the children and from a milliner in town and the children got two pair of stocking each, a pair of gloves each some pretty gingham dresses (which I shall not make up till spring). Vick received a box of blocks and Edie a picture book and a box of doll clothes with a dollie to wear them.

Pres. Phillips took dinner with us last Tuesday and today we take up our notes from McKendree. We expect them now by every mail. This is doing pretty well for this much of a year. Don't you think so? There is every prospect of a prosperous year. There is gradually deepening religious feeling in the church and we hope to start a protracted meeting next week. Pray for us.

I am now helping our dressmaker to make Vick a black velvet cap and cloak. I think he will look swell in it.

We have had a good deal of company lately and really it is a pleasure to have them come in. I feel well enough to work and enjoy it too. I have my washing and scrubbing done and do the rest [myself]. Lonnie helps me a good deal. When I am in a hurry Edie will wash and put away the dishes real nicely. I never call on her when I can help it—for I don't want her to get tired of working before she knows anything about. She can iron towels and such things very neatly for so young a child. I am much pleased with the parsonage. I have a nice parlor well furnished and a bedroom opening into it with a good carpet on the floor and a nice bed in it so that company does not bother me any.

I expect Sister Cline with four of her children here next Monday night. She has a fine little son about five weeks old. I am looking for Mother very soon. I have heard from home several times since I came down here. The last was a letter from Willie *[her younger brother William Winterton Flint]* about ten days ago. He complained that he could not hear from you. Said he guessed you had gone into a torpid state for the winter and was like himself immensely pleased and totally satisfied with your state in life. He seems to be doing well and so does Fletcher *[another Flint brother]*. I think Henry too is on the right track. Have heard but little from Wesley and have not yet seen them. I understand they are doing well and are giving good satisfaction.

The folks at Mt. Olive are all wide awake for business. I think they are doing unusually well if making money fast may be a criterion of prosperity. Well we seem to be all doing something. I forgot to tell you I read an original poem Christmas night. D. W. Phillips asked me if you and I wrote as many essays as we used to when he was a student. He is very pleasant and I enjoyed his visit very much.

I have bought me a new dress and have it made so that it suits me real well. I will send you a sample of it and my cashmere too. I thought I could not afford a cashmere this year but it came all the same. Lonnie gave me a beautiful silk handkerchief for a Christmas gift. How did you fare? Please write soon. L. sends love. Give my love to ester and the boy and Mr. N.

Lovingly Edith

20. ELT to "Uncle Nelson" early 1880s?

[letter from young Edith Laura Thrall, oldest child of LWT and EFT, to "Uncle Nelson," husband of EFT's sister Mary]]

Dear Uncle Nelson

I want to tell you that I love you. Mamma says you have a wee wee little baby at your house. I wish I could see him. Is he pretty? Can he walk?

What is his name? Wont you get his mamma to let you and Aunt Mary
bring him to see us? We buy milk from Mrs. Bunch and we could feed
him. We are going to have a christmas tree here. Are you going to have
one? How do you and Aunt Mary get along? Come and see us

Edie L. Thrall

21. EFT to LWT [probably 1880—1883, as Victor was born 1877 and William 1880]

Ashley

Thursday A.M.

Dear Lonnie,

Your card came yesterday. Was sorry to hear of your disappointment
day before yesterday. I suppose you were busy yesterday. Willie is a little
poorly today. I have prepared Victor's dinner for the picnic and took it
over to Sister Morris. She will attend to him. He will march with his
class if they go out at all.

I really doubt their going for we had a fearful storm here last night. I
had not got to sleep before it began; a little after eleven I think; so I did
not get to sleep until some time after two o'clock. We had three separate
storms. Two trees are broken down in our yard, one large one at
Hammonds and several at Catterdins. A great amount of rain fell.

Fannie Hammond staid with me last night. No word from Edie unless
there is a letter at the office now. Vickie has cried himself to sleep both
nights since you left. He says he has "just such an aching in his *very soul*
now Papa and Edie are both gone." Well I hope to see you tonight and
am sorry you did not get to go to Carbondale. Lovingly,

Edith

22. EFT in Lebanon to LWT, 1882

Lebanon Ill.

Sat. noon

Dear Lonnie

I write you a letter to enclose with the children's letters. I had theirs nearly done when Charlie *[brother-in-law Charles W. Campbell?]* brought me yours of yesterday afternoon. I was not surprised to read of *[illegible]* Walker's death after your letter of yesterday. Well we know he suffered much *[illegible]* and was prepared for the change.

I feel anxious about your health. I know you are apt to suffer from headache after sitting up all night. I hope you rested well last night and feel well this morning. Many thanks for your kind remittance. I am going to buy Victor some new shoes this afternoon. He needs them. Carrie *[Carrie Thrall Campbell, Leonidas's older sister]* and I visited Clio *[McKendree College literary society]* yesterday afternoon. There was a good attendance and some good performances. I regretted very much that a storm came up and hurried us home before the society adjourned.

Alta *[Gould, a Thrall cousin]* is doing real well. Charlie expects to teach either at Alma *[?]* or Ofallon this winter. I don't much think they will go south. I know Carrie don't want to go. I shall think of you tomorrow. I am anxious to know something of your new book of Dr. C. on missions. An Odd Fellows funeral has been gathering for some time and they have just proceeded to the grave. Peter Bussong is the deceased. I wonder how your supplies hold out. I will give you commission on those chicks when I sell them for your care.

We expect to come home Tuesday P.M. by way of Sandoval. If it is cold please bring a shawl or cloak to the depot for Edie and one for me. Willie and Victor are well provided for.

Lovingly,

Edith

23. EFT to Sister Roach 10 November 1882

Grayville Ill.

Nov. 10. 1882

Dear Sister Roach

I hope you are well and happy. We are pretty well at present. I have been sick again, not very bad but it has left me with a wearisome cough an unusual complaint with me. Mr. T. *[LWT]* has gone to Carmi to attend a Sunday School Convention. I should have gone up to visit Mr. T's sisters *[Mary Thrall Morgan, Laura Thrall Gould, and possibly Caroline Thrall Campbell]* but felt afraid to go away and change bed and room. I am so very anxious to get well and strong.

I was not able to go home at the time I intended to go and sister Mary *[Mary Flint Nelson]* came home. Then she and mother *[Mary Gedney Flint]* came down to see me here. They could only stay a few days but I did enjoy their visit so much. We are real well fixed here and the parsonage is so arranged that it is much easier to keep house in it than in the parsonage in Ashley. We have a fireplace in the sitting room and we have about six cords of good wood corded up in the yard.

Our fruit here consists of a large walnut tree and a large persimmon. They are both well loaded with very fine fruit.

On the same block with us resides the Presbyterian minister Bro. Hogg. They reached here the week after we did. They have quite a family, but all the children except seven are married. Four of the married ones live *[in]* the northern part of the state. They are real pleasant folks. I called there this after noon. Took Willie *[William Flint Thrall]*. He grew tired and started off saying "Come, hurry up, your tatoes are burning." I took him home after that speech. He is just the same "little Lillie." He has not forgotten you.

How is Sister Rice and the little boy? Where is Lula? I wish she was teaching school here so Edie *[Edith Laura Thrall]* could go to school to her. I am going to keep Edie at home now. She will take music lessons and can study at home if we think best.
Have you formed the acquaintance of Bro. & Sister Rohrbough? Have you heard Bro. R. preach? How are Alice and Mary? Are you still staying with Sister Pace?

Have you made any arrangments *[sic]* for the winter? I wish you were here tonight. Have wished it many a time since I came here.

We have a pleasant people. They are not much addicted to going to church. They tell us Bro. Carter, who was the preacher last year, sent a postal card to every member of the church inviting them to service and got about half of them there twice. Well Good night Write as soon as you can find time.

Lovingly E. F. Thrall

24. EFT to Sister Roach 17 September 1883

Grayville Ill.

Sept. 17, 1883

Dear Sister Roach

Your letter was received awhile ago. I at that time was very sick but am better now. We are all tolerably well. Mr. T. starts to conference tonight. Will pass through Ashley sometime in the night.

Now will you excuse a brief letter for the present for this is only a business letter. I would like to have you come and spend the winter with me and will tell you some of the circumstances and find out just what you think. You know just what our family is at present. We expect another one sometime during next month. Mr. T. will pay your expenses on the trip if you can come. I have a good washer-woman and should not expect you to do any washing. My sewing is in pretty good shape. Of course there will *[be]* little things to attend to but the bulk of it is done.

Now will you come? Can you write during this week and let me know if you can come and give me some idea of what terms you would like to make? A week from tomorrow I must settle the question with a lady who was here today. She has a child to bring and that you know might not be best.

One reason I have delayed writing was I was anxious to know whether we would remain here or move. *[The decision was in the hands of the regional Methodist conference; ministers usually spent only a year or two in any one church.]* I cannot tell yet, but I think we will move from this house next week.

I suppose Lulie *[Sulie?]* is about to begin her school. Give her my love and tell her I wish her the best of success.

Be sure to let us hear from you this week.

Lovingly

Mrs. E. F. Thrall

[Charles Haven Thrall was born 20 October 1883]

25. EFT to Sister Roach 11 December 1883

Grayville Ill.

Dec. 11 1883

Dear Sister Roach

I wrote to you about two weeks ago and laid my letter on Mr. T.'s table to be posted. Martha went in and cleared up the table putting the letter in his drawer where it has securely rested until just now, while I wondered why you did not write again. I supposed he took it to the office and he was not aware of its existence. Please pardon my long silence on this plea. We were very glad you reached home safely and that things were going on nicely. I hope you are comfortably settled at home for the winter. We are tolerably well here.

I have had a hard time since you left. Baby was four weeks old before I could sit up and I have had several little spells since. Had had "weed in the breast" and bronchitis. Charlie has of course suffered from my poor health. He don't grow very fast but seems real bright. Will laugh and crow when you talk to him and I believe he knows his name. He is a rather fretful baby and requires a great deal of attention. I hope he will do better as I grow stronger and better able to nourish him.

I went to church on Thanksgiving day for the first time since last July. Have been twice since.

You remember we teased you about Bro. Bonner the widower here. Well he went to Carbondale the day before Thanksgiving and came home on the next Saturday with a new wife. So you see you have lost that chance! Excuse me for being so naughty. I like his wife very much. She is a fine singer and a church worker. She was the widow of a railroad conductor.

Edie and Victor are in school and doing well. Willie is trotting around about the same as ever. He thinks ever so much of the baby. Martha does pretty sell. I am so glad that Lula['s] school is so satisfactory.

Will you please see what the chances are for getting gossamers for the children in Ashley. I would not mind the price I would have to pay here if I could get a good article. Please send me word how much they would cost. Lula spoke of getting one. What was it she paid? How did she like the pattern? I have made Edie some by the same pattern and she is much pleased with them. Mother is some better. Love to all my friends.

Please write as soon as you can. We are to have a Christmas tree. Goodbye.

Lovingly yours

Edith F. Thrall

26. EFT to Sister Roach 17 February 1884

Grayville Ill.

February 17 1884

Dear Sister Roach

After so long a silence I will try to send you a few lines. We are all tolerably well. We had to take Edie out of school for a month's rest. She is now up at Bone Gap visiting her aunts and cousins. Vickie is in school and doing real well too. Willie is prancing around much as usual. He is going to Sunday School next summer he says and this *[is]* one thing to look forward to for him. He grows fast and is just about as great a rogue as ever.

Now I suppose you would like to hear about your boy. Well Charlie took to growing when he was about two months old and has kept it up at a good rate. His hair is growing and it is a pretty brown. He knows us all and knows his own name. I shall shorten his clothes in April.

I was so sorry to hear of Thomas Roach's misfortune. It seems as if they were just fairly set up and were beginning to enjoy life when in a simple hour every thing is swept away. Are they trying to keep restaurant again? Did Lula receive that catalogue of McKendree College that Mr. T. sent her?

I suppose her school is now out unless she teaches another term. If she goes to McKendree I hope to see her next May. Some of the *[folks?]* here sent their children to Ewing *[a Baptist academy in Franklin County]* and now have brought them home and some are now attending the common school here because they say it is better than Ewing. Now the fault may be in the young people themselves. I have usually found out that when one really wants to learn they can do *[so]* at nearly any of the schools. I am so glad you are enjoying your pastor this winter. I think he is a very good man.

The high water is the chief topic of conversation here at present. The Wabash *[River]* is very high. I heard today that it has fallen an inch since daylight. It is not quite so high as it was last year. We have had almost incessant rain for the last ten days. This evening the mist is gathering close. I can hardly see over the nearest hills.

There is talk of selling the parsonage next week. If it is sold we shall have to move as soon as we can find a house to move into. I wish they would, for I don't want another preacher's wife to move into this little place.

Give my love to all who may inquire. We often speak of you and wish to see you. Some day we will meet in a better land. Sister Briffitt is very feeble and has been so nearly all winter. I doubt if she lives through the next two *[ten?]* months.

Lovingly,

Edith T.

27. EFT to LWT 15 August 1884

Grayville Ill.

Thurs. 3 P.M. Aug. 15. 1884.

Dear Lonnie

I wonder just where you are now. We reached home all safely. Mr. Mitchell took us up to the parsonage. All was just as I left it. About half an hour after I reached home Minnie Ronalds came around with the buggy and wanted me to go for a ride. Well I went and had a nice ride. We called at Sister Prunty's as we came back. She wanted to know where you was and when you would be home again. Said that nothing had yet been heard from Bro. West. Fannie was expected home tonight—&c. &c.

When I got back to the house I found that Bro. Oliver Dickerman from Ashley had called during my absence. I very much regretted the fact of not seeing him. He complimented Edie on her fast growth and petted Charlie. Said he was a noble little fellow.

It is very warm this afternoon. The children are playing around. They spent a very pleasant night and are willing for us to go to another wedding under the same circumstances. I have felt as well as I could hope to feel. As soon as dinner was over I lay down and slept awhile.

Now I have only time enough to hastily finish this letter and mail it. I hope you will receive it tomorrow. If you see any of our old acquaintances who may remember and inquire after me just give my best wishes. I think I will send a card tomorrow unless I have more news than a card can carry. We will remember you and pray for you. Keep up heart. I hope soon to hear from you. Lovingly Edith

28. EFT to LWT 7 October 1887

Friday Oct 7. 1887.

Dear Lonnie

When I got here yesterday morning I was just in time to get my letter in the mail and then I got your long letter that I enjoyed very much I am glad you are well and enjoying your self so much. I feel really sorry for Mrs. R. She must be having a tedious time of it and then to have moving and all its attendant worries on her mind even if she can't see it done. I know by past experience that it is easier to be able to work than to know the work must be done and be unable to help.

I have studied a great deal about our arrangements in the parsonage. I had been thinking that if we put the old parlor carpet on the sitting room floor it *[would?]* be gone before spring and now we can use it to carpet the parlor bedroom and maybe help one or more of the other rooms and in the bedrooms it will last for several years. That new rag carpet will look pretty on the sitting room floor for this winter anyway. Now I may change my plan when I see the house but this is my present idea.

I would not advise you to buy any more wood stoves. The coal as you *[know?]* is cheaper and it will be easier for you and Victor and there will be enough wood cutting to fill the two we already have. I am inclined to think you had better buy a sofa for the parlor, we really need it. Dont buy a table till I come. I am not at all certain that we shall need it. Do as you please about buying chairs before I come.

My present plan is to come on Wednesday. I can then bring the children with their clothes all clean and tidy. I am now at Lizzies *[Morgans]* and will remain in Bone Gap until Sunday and spend the rest of the time at

Laura's *[Goulds]*. Solon is quite sick with his rheumatism. Crete *[Laura's daughter]* will go to Evanston next week.

I have had a sore mouth and it is now well except one sore on the right side in the upper part of the throat and that feels like it had a splinter in it and bothers me about swallowing. When I swallow it pains my right ear as well as my throat.

We had a very pleasant visit at Aunt Potamia's yesterday. Lizzie, Laura and me with the three little boys.

I am pained as well as surprised at some things in a part of your letter. I hope things may not be quite so bad. I guess you will have a chance to see how they conduct weddings before you are called on to officiate at one. Crete is very anxious to know if it is Miss Carrie McGerrin *[?]* who is to be married for she is *[illegible]* of Crete's. Well dear goodby. It is now about mail time so I must send this off. The children are all well. Lovingly Edith

29. EFT to LWT perhaps late 1880s

[undated page 3 of a letter relating to son Charles born 1883]

Thank you for them. It seems to me that you have a good seat. I know you have been very busy the last few days and you have been good to write to us. We enjoy your letters so much. The house beside us is going to be very pretty. It will have two porches both looking toward our house. Prof. Johnson comes to see it every day. I hope they will move into it.

I went with Charlie to the doctor yesterday. He showed me the unnatural growth but says it is dead now and we are drawing it out with the flaxseed poultices. It is very clear to us and is black now. He says there will always be something of a scar.

The plaster *[poultice?]* burned so badly yesterday morning that he could not keep still and he told me he knew of a lady here who had such lovely plants would I give him a nickel to buy a slip of sweet geraniums. Of course he got it, and came home very soon with slips for fifteen varieties of plants and "She would not take my nickel." He spent all the morning potting his plants and it kept his mind from his pain.

30. EFT in Salem to ELT in Lebanon 10 October 1889

Salem Ill

Thursday noon

Dear Edie

Your letter came yesterday and as I was writing to Papa I just slipped it in his letter and it is now in Carbondale. I shall only be able to write you a little. Had a long letter from Papa this morning. No definite news but lots of gossip.

Don't both about that collar pattern. I have made one myself that answered very well. I have bought me a new calico dress will send you a piece if I can. Have Willie's and Charlie's woolen waists done and they are very nice. Guess Vick wont get any.

Miss Belle sent your album home without writing in it but she sent with it another album for you a new one with a few words from herself and Miss Georgle. [?] The album is pretty and so are their contributions. Shall I send the new one to Minnie H. or the old one. Send me word as soon as you can.

They talk of organizing a quartet choir here. That will leave the Deakins [?] out but I don't know how it will turn out. Papa was paid up before he went to conf[erence]. Mrs. Porter has gone to conf and Mrs. Castle and Mrs. Hayn. I am trying to do some house cleaning.

Loving,

Mamma

31. EFT in Greenville to ELT 4 November 1889 Greenville III

Nov 4 1889

Dear Edith

I will send a note with the little boy's letters. I have been very busy today. Have been at work on my dining room carpet this afternoon. Hope to get it down before dinner tomorrow. I have been requested to be at home from one o'clock until six next Wednesday P.M. so I suppose I shall have callers then. Had one this afternoon, a Mrs. Floyd. I am glad you are able to honor the drafts Clio sees fit to make on you. It will do you good. I wonder if you can send to the city for your underclothing! Can Uncle Fletcher *[EFT's brother]* do any trading in St. Louis? I think you ought to have two new undershirts or vests they call them. You are well provided with flannel skirts to I think you can do with the drawers you have unless they are worn out. We think you have been real careful with your money. I am glad of it for money is going to be scarce. This has been a very expensive move for us. Love to Grandma and the rest. Lovingly Mamma.

32. LWT in Greenville to ELT in Lebanon, 24 January 1890

Dear Edie

I guess you think we are a long time writing but we have all been sick. Mamma and I have been sick all the week. I was sick last week, so was she but we got better and I preached Sunday but we both got worse and have had the doctor all of the week. We both better. Mamma is up but does not go out into the kitchen yet. She has a pain all the time in her right lung where she had the abscess a few years ago.

Charlie and Hallie are both poorly. Charlie started to school Monday but was not well enough to continue and has stayed home the latter part of the week. We did not continue the meeting after the week of prayer the weather was so bad and many sick. Willie is expecting to be promoted into the *[?]* grade next Monday. Victor did expect it but he has been sick so much of the time this month that he no longer hopes for it.

[change of handwriting to EFT]

We are very anxious to hear from you but we can hardly expect it until we write. Papa got tired and quit a little while ago so I began. Poor little Hallie is lying on the boy's bed moaning with the headache. We fixed up your bed and brought it down and set it up in the sitting room. I wanted the boys near us this cold weather.

Mrs. Dann sent me a nice comfort one day this week. It is all made of new calico and is quite pretty. I think grandma has been very quick in her work with her work in making up those pieces so soon. I guess I will have the lining ready. Vickie and Willie have had nearly all the work to do this week. Papa helped them today and I made up the beds in this room today. I hope soon to be well.

Please write

Your Loving Mamma. Love to all the folks.

33. EFT in Lebanon to ELT in Greenville 3 June 1890

Greenville Ill. *[? More likely written from Lebanon]*

Tues. afternoon June 3, 90

Dear Children

Papa got here last night dripping wet having been caught in a heavy rain. He and Willie were just as wet as they could be. Willie had clothes to change but papa had none. He put on an overcoat of Uncle Henry's and as soon as supper was over he went to bed and I dried his clothes. I gave him a quinine pill and this morning he is all right but for a slight cold and sore throat. He was better this noon when he came home from the board meeting.

I have heard that Bro. Headman is likely to be one of the professors next year. We will know soon I guess. The exhibitions were very good they say. I did not get out to either of them. I went Sunday morning to hear the sermon. Dr. Masden did not come and Prof. Jepson made an address to the class. This was very nice. I did not go out at night. I hope you had a nice time at the entertainment last night.

Have you got your new dress done yet? I saw quite a number of the girls Sunday and they all asked after you Edie. Several of them said they were going to write to you as soon as this busy week was over.

I cant write any more for it is nearly mail time and I must get this in. Tell Willie he may go barefoot if he will let you tell him when to take his shoes off and when to put them on and you must be good watchful of him for you know his lungs are not very strong and that whooping cough hangs on him so. Give my love to all the little boys. We will soon be home to see you.

Lovingly Mamma

34. LWT (in Greenville?) to ELT (in Lebanon?) autumn, perhaps 1890

Thursday 11 A.M.

Dear Edie

Mamma received your letter this morning. She is more crowded with work today than I so I will write.

I got home at 9 P.M. Monday. Had to walk from Smithboro as the train on the Jacksonville road changed time that day and made me miss at Smithboro. *[about 5 miles to Greenville]* We are all well.

Are reconstructing things a little in this old mansion. We have moved our bed up stairs this A.M. Mamma has invented a way of carpeting one of the big rooms entire and we have concluded to make it the lower one and I shall move my study into it and try and fix up a little down there and have the large upstairs room that I have been using for a study vacant. How do you like it? We shall put that big bureau in the back part of the hall (down stairs) and the single bed in my study to relieve the rocking chair occasionally. We shall not buy any carpet but may buy another hanging lamp. We are going up town after dinner to see what we can find in the way of a clock for you. Every one seems to receive us back kindly. I saw Lizzie Morgan and Al. at Conf. but none of Solon's folks. I did not go over there.

Mamma and I went over to Mrs. Bennett's last night after supper and while we were away Mrs. Frank Seaman and Mrs. Evans called here. Yesterday afternoon Mr. Soulsby came and took us buggy riding and then showed us through his new house and by that time Josie came home and we had a croquet game on their ground. Mrs. S. & I beat Mamma and Josie once and they beat us once—then it was time for us to come home.

The boys get on well in school. I am glad you have a Greek Prof. that requires accuracy. To be moderately accurate in Greek is like eating a *moderately* sound egg.

Some surprise is manifest here in learning that Bro Groves has moved from Belleville to Cairo. I have received $18 on my old claim since coming here. About $75 due yet. I guess I will get most of it but I should be pretty glad to see it. Wesley is well pleased with his charge.

We organized an "Itinerant's Club" at Conference. It consists of all the preachers who are in their four years course of study and all the examiners—about 45 of us altogether. Fred Thompson is President and Wesley Flint & Bro Orr of Carlyle and myself are the Executive Committee. We have planned a three days session some time in July or August for Normal work and Lectures on the course of study. A pretty big thing if successfully managed but we are all "green" at it yet.

Now it is about dinner time—the boys are home. I bought a big "punkin" yesterday and mamma has promised us 30 pies out of it. Goodby write often. WE shall expect another letter at breakfast time next Tuesday if not sooner.

Lovingly

Papa

I wrote to you from Conf. I suppose you received it—

3 P.M. We have just been uptown and bought you a jacket. We came home by way of the Express Office and expressed it to your address. It ought to be there as soon as this letter—Write soon and let us know that you got. We also bought Hallie a pretty suit.

35. Undated from LWT, perhaps early 1890s

Effingham 9 A.M. Saturday

Dear Wife and Children

I did not intend to write this morning but I am going to Bro Sale's—one mile in the country to dinner and they may not bring me back in time to get a letter out tonight.

I went to Salem, went first to Harriet Marshal's. Found quite a hospital. The preacher and John *[Stonecipher?]* sick and Mrs. Marshal very sick. She fell Wed morning and struck her head against the stone steps and became unconscious. She is thought to be better but is in a serious condition. She was in such a nervous condition in the forenoon that I was not allowed to see her but was asked to call in the P.M. which I did and it happened *[at]* a time when they had just got her to sleep so I did not see her at all.

Ella Marshal is there and Mrs. Davenport. I went to the church to call on the preacher—not so sick but that he had gone down there though he is quite poorly—and went to Sister Thompsons where I received my first invitation to dinner. I was glad enough to accept it and stayed in the kitchen and talked to Mrs. Thompson while she cooked it. She had a sewing woman there. The whole family sat down to dinner at once. Bess managed to get Will and Grace loose at the same time and she shut up her store long enough to come, then Lottie hurried back and opened up.

Mrs. Thompson has bought the lot between the parsonage and Ben Martins residence and is going to build right away. The Trustees sold her a 10 ft strip off the east side of the parsonage lot so she will have a 60 ft front and it will all reach clear through to the back street. The house will stand back about on a line with the parsonage and Ben Martin's residence.

After dinner I went down to see Sister Whitten but the house was shut up and no one at home. I called at Dr. Young's. One of the boys is very dangerously ill. I called at Utterbacks on way to depot. Charlie took dinner there and then went with some boys out to Mrs. Grankonner's.

Preached here to a full house last night. The *[?]* preacher was here to see me yesterday and missed me. Some of his people were here and

49

interviewed me last night. I want to get out there but if it is very *[?]* I do not know that I will. I am feeling quite well. Goodby—

Lovingly

Papa

36. EFT in Lebanon to LWT 30 May, probably 1890s

Lebanon Ill

Friday evening 3 oclo[ck]

Dear Lonnie

I received your letter this morning and was real glad to hear from you and know that you are all well. We are getting along nicely. Harry *[HLT?]* is much better of his cough. Mother came home at nine oclock last night. *[News of her brothers:]* Jim is getting better slowly. Fletcher has an offer of a situation in a large wholesale drug firm in St. Louis. He is there today and if suitable terms can be made he will go in their employ. As soon as Brooks brothers heard of this position open they came to Fletcher and told him that if he would remain with them they would give him a permanent situation if he would accept it. I don't know which he will take. If he leaves the place at Brooks open, it may be that Willie will try it awhile if he is able to stand it.

I went out to the graveyard with Mother a little while this afternoon. We took a basket of flowers and laid them on Father's grave. Then we came home and Willie, Carrie and Harold are there now. John Baker speaks and a man named Smith. I saw Bro. West, John Chamberlain and Professor Jepson.

I have been told that if Bro. W. is removed from this charge he will leave the conference, that he is very anxious to go away. This is "sub rosa."

I think that many people are expected here next week. Genevieve Jepson has the valedictory.

Wesley cannot come to commencement. I am disappointed for I hoped to see him. Mother says they are doing very well. Have found quite a lot of rich relations at Alton and they are real good to them. One family of said relations pay two hundred dollars to the salary. The lady is a successful S.S. teacher and early in April she came down to the parsonage and gave Zie and Minnie each ten dollars to help buy their spring clothes and all this help you know.

Dr. C. P. Masden of St. Louis will preach the Baccalaureate sermon next Sunday morning. I hope you will have a pleasant day and the same on Sunday. Goodby dear for today.

Lovingly

Edith

37. EFT in Greenville to ELT in Lebanon 16 September 1892

Greenville Ill

Sept 16. 1892.

Dear Edith

I am here alone this afternoon for a little while. Papa is out working on the parsonage subscription and Vickie is out trying to find out something about that social that is to come off tonight.

Papa is not at all well. Yesterday I was worse than the day you left. Had fever and dozed the afternoon stupidly away. I am better today and think I am fairly on the way to get well. Charlie fretted all night last night with festering toe.

About the time your train left Wed. afternoon Mr. Morris who lives right by us came and asked papa to be at his house at seven to marry a couple. It was a very pretty wedding I am told and I have a new "five" tucked snugly away. It will buy some flannel and an undershirt for papa.

We have a book of plans for a parsonage came today. Papa and I have agreed on one that will cost from $1000 to $1200. Vickie leans to another at the same price but on a different plan. I have not touched a needle since you went away, but I must soon get to work a something

[remaining pages missing]

38. EFT in Greenville to ELT 28 September 1892

Greenville Ill

Sept 28 1892

Dear Edith

Your letter came yesterday morning. I was real glad to hear from you. Papa went to conference yesterday and today I had a card from him. He was nearly through with his work with the examinations. I am so glad you are going to conference. I hope you will enjoy it, and you will get to see Aunt Zie. I wish I could see her. Give her my love and tell [her] to write to me.

I went to the missionary meeting this afternoon at Mrs. Savage's. Mrs. Sparkes took me over. The salary is not all paid yet but I think it will be in a few days. Gov & Mrs Fifer *[of Illinois]* have invited the ladies who are to be in attendance at the North Western Branch W.F.M.S. *[Women's Foreign Missionary Society]* at Springfield to a reception to be given at their residence on the evening of the 11th of next month. I hope I shall be able to go.

Victor is very much pleased with the college. He likes the teachers very much. The work at present is nearly all done by two professors; a brother of the president and Miss Shay. They take turn about in conducting prayers. They have a students prayer meeting on Fri night. Victor studies Latin, Greek and Physical Geography. I have fixed up my silk dress and have my black cashmere about done. I guess you was about tired out last Sat. after doing both washing and ironing. Do you get any stronger?

It would be so nice if you should have Kate for a chum next term. Where does she board now? What classes does Genevieve teach?

So far as I am concerned I do not feel like subscribing for the "Repos." We are so close run for money that I cannot see the way clear. You can speak to Papa when you see him Sun. if you think of it.

I do have a time of it with poor Mrs. Jones. She took a spell of screaming at me from that little upper room yesterday. She ought to be sent to the asylum where something might be done for her. She came over this morning and begged some cloves [?] but did not sit down. Old brother Buchanan who lives near Mrs. Weise is about to die. There are several new cases of typhoid fever in town but none serious.

You spoke of the funeral of Bruce Yaggart. I used to go to S.S. with him [when] I was a little girl.

They have not begun work on the parsonage yet but are still studying plans. I heard Mon. that they were to begin next week. Miss May McGowan is building a house on that vacant block next Mrs. Frank Seaman. Mrs. Dr. Allen is building two houses and Ward Reid one. I think the building is what we need.

Please write out Aunt Carrie's recipe for baked beans and send it in your next. I think I will send to St. Louis & buy my underclothing ready made. I am getting along very well now with the work. I don't know how we will do about the house cleaning but we will get through some way. Please write soon. Give my love to all. I hope uncle Henry is well again.

Lovingly

Mamma

39. HLT (age 7) in Greenville to ELT in Lebanon, 2 November 1892

Postmarked 5 pm

Dear Edith

How are the folks. They have began the parrinage [parsonage] near toward done. We have a horse and buggy. I get lots of rides. If the roads

53

are good Vickie says he is going to take you and Kate riding when you come next Thanksgiving.

Can Toddy *[?]* Bogan count 20? Do you get your lessons well? and will you get 100 on deportment? I did today. Charlie cleans out the barn very well. Willie takes care of Mrs. Saulsbury's *[hens? horses?]* for 25 cents a week.

What are you going to do with all your bugs? Will you bring them home to decorate the new parlor? I will send you a picture of the floor of the new house. *[diagram]* Then there will be three bedrooms upstairs.

Hallie Thrall

40. EFT to ELT 2 November 1892

Wednesday noon

Dear Edith

Your card was received this morning and we were much relieved to hear the hopeful word from grandma. Yesterday morning the little boys had their letters ready so I sent them off. Hallie sent you a plan of the house. I will send you a few more particulars. The kitchen and dining room are only one story. The house is very much like Frank Seamans as seen from the outside but is higher making the upper rooms more airy.

They are going to make a large cistern and there is a good cellar under the kitchen with an entrance from the back porch. There will be sliding doors between the bedroom and sitting room and one large sliding door between the parlor and the sitting room. *The doors will be there not just the spaces.*

The Junior League will give a missionary sociable next Monday night in the church I guess. The Epworth League has undertaken to raise $50.00 for the parsonage and they have laid it on the departments to raise about ten dollars each. Etta Kirkham's dep. will give a social a week from Fri night at Mrs. Evan's and will have what the Metropolis folks called a Muggins Junction by way of refreshments. We are hoping for a grand success.

Miss Wright of the public school is becoming quite prominent in Jun. Le. *[Junior League?]* work. The W. C. T. U. *[Women's Christian Temperance Union]* are giving monthly socials. Their first was given at Mrs. Grube's last Fri. night. There was ten cents admission fee and over one hundred present. We could not be there for it was the night of the reception at Bennetts. We are not having a very good attendance at the League Sun afternoon at least not as good as we wish for. Hope to do better soon.

Vickie is still doing well at college. He was sitting studying his greek lesson one evening when I heard him exclaim "I would not be caught dead with the greek accusative" so you know that some of his troubles are. Write at once. Love to mother.

Yours

Mamma

41. EFT in Greenville to ELT 7 November 1892

Greenville Ill. Nov. *[postmarked 5 pm]*

Dear Edith

Your letter came this morning. We are all so glad that grandma is better. I have not seen any of Uncle George *[Flint]*'s folks today except as Earl stopped on the walk this morning for Harry. *[First cousins, of an age]* We are tolerably well. I could not go out yesterday and my lungs hurt me so I have to be careful, but I think I am improving.

Mrs. Laws died last Thursday evening just before nine oclock. I was there two hours before she died and she spoke to me. Mrs. Hare (the widow) is very sick.

Our League social is progressing nicely. Etta was here a few minutes ago. Wish you could be here with us. Our L. M. *[?]* went off all right. The parsonage is progressing. They hoped to set the painter at work next Wed. but I guess the rain of yesterday will interfere some with that. The roof is partly on.

I will send those books as soon as I can get them together. If you want a book on Egypt we can send you a book we have here, a small one but reliable. You know it. I rather think Egypt would be the basis of a more scholarly oration than any of the others but it would require considerable research to do it justice.

Dr Warren's address will help you to something more adapted to the age we live in and the purpose for which we are living. Willie says "Tell Edie to write on Egypt." Victor says tell her to write on "Four hundred years of American civilization." He wrote an essay on that for the first ex. *[examination?]* given in the G. College and won considerable commendation for it. They take the first steps this afternoon toward organizing a literary society. We bought our horse and buggy from Rob. Wilson and paid $110.00 for it. Vickie says Nell gets prettier every day.

Aunt Carrie's address is Glenwood, Mo. Did you notice her article of Junior Work in the Epworth Herald about a month or more ago? Tell Uncle Willie we will some of us write to him soon. We hope to send you "some money from home" this week. Tell Kate I hope the pamphlet will help her. I hope to hear soon that your underclothing *[is]* made it is getting too cold to be without it and it may turn real cold any time. Try to get them done right away. We hope to move in about three or four weeks.

Love to all

Mamma

42. EFT to ELT 15 January 1893, on printed stationery: L. W. Thrall, A.M., Pastor M.E. Church, Greenville

Dear Edith

I have been so busy since you went home that I have not written anything, I don't know that I have any thing much done to show for it save lots of dishes was washed floors swept, meals cooked and mending done. I don't keep up with my mending letting alone making any thing new.

Well it has been so cold that it is very hard to do anything. We have a stove put up in the dining room and I shall put in some furniture tomorrow. Have not got the bed room fixed yet. They have not done any more work in that room and I don't know when they will. As soon as the weather moderates a little I shall fix up the bed room and then let the two rooms upstairs that are unfurnished remain so until nearer spring.

I have felt so anxious about your head rig while it is so cold I want you to get something warmer. I think we will be able to send you some money in this letter. I have not seen anything of Della Bradford since you went back. I don't see many folks out here as yet. Nobody drops in for there is scarcely any body we know who lives about here. I guess they are waiting for us to get fixed up and then they will come.

Mrs and her Samson called one day. They have bought a new horse. Mrs. Jennie Seaman came in to see me on missionary work. The Editor of the *Heathen Woman's Friend* is dead. She has edited the paper for 22 years; ever since it was founded. Two of our near neighbors have called. Mrs. Maxey and Mrs. Harris.

I will tell you a funny little experience we had. A day or two after you left we heard peculiar noises about the house. It sounded as if someone was dragging light pieces of wood around in those unoccupied rooms upstairs. It continued all through the night and the next day. After listening and watching we then found out that it was the window weights swinging between the walls. About the time we found out what it was it ceased & although we have had high winds since[,] we have had no more such noises.

I have had some trouble with my throat. It feels as if the sharp edge of a tooth had cut my tongue and the inflammation had extended down my throat. It troubles me a great deal. I think some of going to the Dr. and find out what is the matter. Charlie has been sick and out of school for two days. Has a bad cold, and cough. Harry coughs considerable too so I have brought them down stairs to sleep.

The League gave a social at Mrs. Weise last Fri night and made between eleven and twelve dollars on their parsonage sub. Please write soon and tell all the news. Give my love to all and send word how Uncle Will gets along with Dr. Hayes.

Lovingly, Mamma

43. CHT to ELT, same Greenville stationery, 16 January 1893

Dear Edith:

I received your letter before the holidays and sorry that I did not answer it sooner. I have not been feeling very well the last week or so. I have to sleep on the sofa with Hallie. Mamma has bought some little round dover powders for us and they look almost like little pills. I took one of them and found that they were bitter.

There was an Epworth League social at Weise and you had to pay a dime to get in and they had a fish pond where we would go and pay another dime and take a stick with a string and bent pin and throw it over a curtain in one corner of a room and pull it out and get some little toys or some candy. Victor took Nannie Martin with him. Will got a stick of candy. Joadie, *[?]* Mamma and I did not go. Well it is getting late and I am sleepy and have got tired. Send my love to all. Write soon,

Your Pet Charlie

44. LWT to ELT, same Greenville stationery 19 January 1893

Dear Edith

Mamma *[EFT]* has just received your letter. It finds us all about as well as usual only Mamma's throat and mouth. She is going up this P.M. to have some teeth drawn which the Dr says are the cause of the trouble.

The Epworth League elected officers last night. Mamma is President. Etta K. & Kate M. have their old places of 1st & 4th Vice. Miss Wright has Literary and Mrs. Della Bradford the Mercy & Help Departments. Gesie *[?]* S. is Secretary and Della Bradsly Treasurer. John Bradford is S.S. Supt and making a good one.

Victor is going to work for Harry Ferguson this summer in the farm near Reno *[eight miles northeast of Greenville in Bond County]*. He gets $14 per month. He will begin as soon as present College term closes —

about March 23 and continue till fall work is done. What do you think of that?

I am glad to hear of the move at L. toward paying off the debt. There is also a notice of it in the central *[Methodist newspaper?]* this week. By the way I have sent the largest list of Centrals ever sent from this charge. Now I am going to hitch up and take Mamma to Dentist. Goodbye

Lovingly, Papa

45. LWT to ELT, same Greenville stationery 7 February 1893

Dear Edith

Your letter to Mamma came this morning. You must have got a pretty hard jolt. I have fallen a few times but no damages.

We had a very good Quarterly Meeting for the weather. Quar. Conf. passed off pleasantly. I had said nothing more about salary but when it came up they fixed it at $900 unanimously. That will make us better off than last year by nine months house rent and will make the salary as we shall have to report it to Conf. $975. Well to *raise* it is another thing but I think they will succeed. I enclose $15 draft to pay on Board. There will be some more after a while.

The Campbellites are still having a big time. About 40 accessions. They expect to close the meeting tonight.

We have at last put the carpet down in the down-stairs bedroom and have got straitened out some.

We have organized an Epworth Reading Club. Meets Monday night at private houses. Have organized Teachers' meeting. Have it Wednesday night at the church.

We are sorry to hear about Rebecca. We are all about as usual Mamma's jin *[chin?]* is still sore on the right side but the left is about well. Hallie had a little toothache this P.M. and as it is a very cold one we kept him home from school. He is playing around though now. Mamma said she will write to you soon. WE have not got anything from the papers about the society matter you spoke of—

Goodbye, Lovingly, Papa

46. EFT to ELT, same Greenville stationery, 5 March 1893

Dear Edith

Your letter came today and we were very glad to hear from you. I am glad to say we are all better today. Vickie went back to work this afternoon. He is not real well and looks thin. I hope he will improve. I have not been out in town for more than two weeks. I am sorry the book was wrong and will send the other tomorrow.

I am glad Uncle Willie is doing so well. He has had enough rough sailing, it seems as if it was time his fortunes took a turn. I have always thought he would do well at that kind of work.

Did Charlie have the measles? You thought some time ago that he had been exposed to the disease. I never saw a more complete sweep in any house than we had here. We were all sick here and then Vickie came home Sat. and he was sick too.

This is the boy's holiday week and I am glad of it. Kites are all the fashion now and every boy you see has his eyes turned up to "the blue". Willie has taken to making kites to trade with the other boys. Don't you feel astonished?

The little poem was Charlie's. Last week he had trouble in finding a piece to speak and so spoke his own composition and was marked 98 on it. Rather a youthful author! Della Bradford is at the Hot Springs in Arkansas. She went a week ago today. John had been a week or so and wrote to her that he was not so well so she went right away.

Unless the missionary convention is held at Lebanon I don't think I shall be able to go. There are so many things in the way. I think you was quite a genius to fix up your *[pages missing]*

47. LWT to ELT, same Greenville stationery, 27 March 1893

Dear Edie

We got your letter promptly. I expect you looked for answer before this time but we have all been just poorly and did not have any money to send you till today anyhow. I can only send you $5 just now. I know it is not enough but I will try to send more next week. You will have to stand somebody off either for tuition or books which ever you prefer of the two evils. Or if you are homesick and prefer to come home for this time you may do that. You are always welcome.

Victor went to the farm last Thursday. He started at 11 A.M. in a four horse wagon through the rain. It is about nine miles out there. We look for him home for Easter. We are going to have an Easter Missionary Service Sunday A.M. and take the annual collection. There is a fine prospect now of getting the saloons out. The election is three weeks from tomorrow.

Willie is improving some and is real good about the housework. He is not yet able to go to school. Dr. Easily is treating him. Mamma has been quite poorly for several days with Bronchitis. Friday she did not leave the bed at all but most days she gets about some. She has some Asthma and some heart trouble but all apparently excited by the hard coughing the result of a severe cold and some over exertion.

I have a severe cold and cough but keep going. Preached at a missionary sermon yesterday A.M. but did not make much headway. At night it was Union Temperance Service and Dr. Collins gave us a good one. The Baptist revival is still going on with some encouraging results.

Charlie is taking the whole care of Nellie except currying and Harold helps Willie wash dishes when he gets time.

This is the last day on a $210 parsonage debt and I have to hustle to collect it up. I don't feel a bit like it either. Victor got 100 in Algebra and 76 in Latin, 78 in Greek. He hated to leave home this time poor boy. Mamma is writing to him now. The prospects are not very brilliant for the Woman's Missionary Convention to be held in Lebanon. Mrs. Hyps *[Hypes?]* wants it somewhere else. So I guess Mamma will not get to L.

Let us hear from you.

Lovingly

Papa

48. EFT to ELT, first page(s) missing, postmarked April 1893

[missing pages] old hat so successfully. I wonder if you can make your spring hat do awhile? Dr. Collins the Campbellite preacher is engaged to deliver a series of temperance lectures here to try and help the temperance people carry the election. He was to have given them last week but has postponed them until next week. Some of his members who are in favor of license are objecting so he may fail to give them. I have not much faith in him anyway.

Jonathan Seaman is the temperance candidate for mayor and Akhurst is the license candidate. Our election is on the seventeenth of this month. I feel anxious about Mother *[Mary (Gedney) Flint]*. What seems to be the trouble? I do want to come and see her so much but I guess I will hardly do so until after commencement.

As soon as I am well enough to manage the matter I am going to get a woman to help me and take up the carpet from the sitting room and dining room. There has been so much mud that they are too dusty to lie any longer than necessary. I am like you on having many things planned to do next year if we live and have reasonable health. It is time to get dinner

Lovingly

Mamma

49. Uncle William Winterton Flint in Lebanon to ELT in Greenville, 6 September 1893, *on letterhead of the Trenton Publishing Company (Trenton Herald, $1.50 per year and The Presbyterian, One Dollar per year)*

Lebanon, Illinois, Sept. 6, 1893

Dear Niece:

Your letter is not yet answered so I will use part of this hot, dry, burning, parching, wasting, boiling, frying, drying, dusty afternoon in writing you a short letter. I suppose Vickie and Charlie arrived home safely. I forgot to tell them to report and I guess they have been too busy since to write. We enjoyed their visit very much, and it was owing to my persuasion that they stayed until Wednesday.

This leaves us as well as usual. The heat is hard on Mother, but she keeps up and going. Carrie [and] Charlie keep well and I am about the same as I have been for a few years or so.

Carrie & Charlie and I left here last Thursday afternoon at P.M. and arrived in Cincinnati at 7 A.M. Friday. We left there at 8:26 A.M. on Saturday and arrived here at 6 P.M. So you see we were gone just 48 hrs.

Dr. Amick says I am a kind of curiosity—my right and left lung being as differently affected as though they belonged to two different persons. My right lung is asthmatic and my left is partially solidified, but says his treatment for asthma will cure both. He gave me a thirty days treatment which he claims should do the work. He said however that it might take longer to clear up the left one. We visited the Zoological Gardens and saw some sights worth seeing.

People are in town looking for rooms for students, which looks like business. I am told that the prospects are good for college. Have not seen the new professor yet. I will. Prof. Waggoner and Uncle are at home. I have not seen Mrs. W.

News is quite scarce in town. There seems to be nothing going on. Mrs. Chauberlieu *[Chamberlain?]* is improving. No one else sick, dead, married, or anything else of interest. We have no late word from any of the family circle. Maurie *[?]* Beck and her mother will be home from Colorado this week. How is Mr. Hau? *[?]*

63

Write to us.

Love to all, Your Uncle Will

I will send that Journal

50. CHT to ELT, undated, probably fall 1893, move from Greenville to Salem?

Dear Edie

I will be glad when you come home. We are nearly fixed up. I have a cat & am going to sleep on *[line obscured]* the boy's room upstairs. There is another room opening into their room that I guess will be yours and mine when you get here. We have a big grape arbor and apples and cherries and plum trees, a chicken yard and a barn.

There is a little sled and a big sleigh in the barn. There is a well in the barn yard and there was two cisterns by the house until this afternoon and then one of them caved in and the pump went down and the water is nearly to the top and it looks awful bad. Some men are coming tomorrow to fill it up.

From Charlie

51. EFT in Lebanon to ELT in Salem 15 January 1894

Dear Edith and the Boys

I received your letter last Sat. and intended to write this afternoon but I have had so much company that I did not get any more done than to address the envelope. Mother has been very sick that I have spent my time in her room.

Last Saturday morning she was so bad that I was afraid she would never be any better. Sunday morning she seemed a little better and I went to church in the morning to be present at the memorial service of Dr. Allyn. The service was very impressive. Mrs. E. A. Hypes came up. After I came home I found her very sick. I have not left the house since.

She has been very sick indeed. She began to get better this morning but Oh she is so weak and her cough is so bad except when under the influence of medicine. It is the exhaustion following the grip. I don't know if she will ever be well. I expect to be home Sat unless she is worse.

Josie Otwell came down tonight, and I had quite a long talk with her. Addie is studying Greek too. They all want to go to rooming. If you should happen to be together next spring what [a] literary set you would be!

Prof Barr said he was coming down to see me and Etta Root too. I heard [today?] that rooms could be had at Mrs. Thatchers. Also at old Mr. Peaches near Headmans. I have seen two vacant houses. One the Eckert house on Main St near Mills house, the other Hoyt's residence. I don't know whether either of them are for rent nor the rent expected if they are in the market. The Kirk house is full. A club has its headquarters there. I hope to get considerable information from Barr when he comes.

I can't go round much for I cant leave Mother long. If I see or hear more I will write it. If you get any letters for me from Greenville you may open them. Hope Vickie's cold is better. Charlie said "Tell 'em I'm's all right." I am afraid there is not very much furniture here for Mrs. Beck got lots of things when she went to housekeeping. Write soon to

Mamma

This morning Mother is still better.

52. EFT in Salem to ELT 16 April 1894

Dear Edith

Your letter came this morning glad to hear from you. I start to Altamont tomorrow A.M. on the second train. Papa will home about ten oclock tomorrow and he will take care of the boys. Miss Ketring is just good as she can be. She will be in Lebanon three weeks from tomorrow night May 8th. Don't fail to hear her. I spoke to her of you and Victor and she will be on the lookout for you. Our Thank Offering (thanks to her) will be over thirty dollars. The R. T. of Y. have a quartette from Canada here this week. They sang for us yesterday and one of them preached last night. They are fine singers and good Christian men too.

I hardly get any sewing done at all. The housework mending and company just fill my time. I have a long letter from Mrs. Seaman quite lately. Henry Hair is better and his family are going to him in the south. I want to come after Mother next week if I can but cant be sure yet. I will write to her after I get home this week. Hurrah for Victor and the Platos. I would have said as much for the Philos if he had gone there. Tell him I found a "Farthing" in the house last Friday and "more" too. Tomorrow is election day here and folks are all alert. The fight will be a strong one.

Tell Victor I can't send him a present on his birthday but will send it soon. Caps and gowns and a junior tree! What next? I must close this letter or I will miss the mail. *[Do write?]* more and oftener. Love to all from

Mamma

Edith F. Thrall

53. EFT in Salem to ELT, probably in Lebanon, 6 May 1894

Dear Edith

Grandma has just gone to bed. Willie is at Church and Charlie and Harold are here with me.

We got home all right. Grandma stood the trip much better than we expected and seemed real well yesterday. Not quite so well today. The storm disturbed her last night and she did not seem so well.

We ate lettuce from our garden today and our radishes are doing fine. I have 29 little chickens and will set a hen tomorrow and don't think I will set any more.

I shall be glad when you get home. I am very well pleased with your surroundings so far as I could see. I wonder how Vickie enjoyed his service this afternoon?

The League wants me to go to the convention at Effingham but I don't expect to go. Bro. Marshall feels real spunky because they have not assigned any part to the Salem League, and says he will not attend the convention. We will have a cabinet meeting here tomorrow afternoon to discuss the situation.

Monday night. We held our meeting and I don't know that we are in much better fix than we were before. They say if I will go to the convention I will be able to assume all their work and that I am free from complications but I don't see any way for that to be done. I have had a headache all day and noise this evening with the children all together has worn me almost out. Tell Victor I will write to him a separate letter in a few days.

This is Wednesday morning. I have waited till this time so that I might send you some money. I send you ten dollars. Will send more as soon as possible. I may not be able *[to]* send quite up to date for you know there are some thin quarterly meetings about this time. We had such a good meeting at the League last night. Next Sunday night we conduct the service in the church. Mrs. Thompson has promised to prepare a paper on the "League as foreshadowed in the home teaching of Susannah Wesley."

I am going up town now to see about a new hat for myself and Mother too. Let us hear soon and send a sample of your dress. I approve of your plan of sending to the city and am glad you have so good a chance. Mother says tell you she is just about the same *[as]* she was when at home. She is mending for Charlie.

Mamma

54. EFT in Salem to ELT, probably in Lebanon, 4 June 1894

Dear Edith

Your letter came all right except the sample of your dress but never mind for I will see the dress soon. I will send the money by Papa. I am glad you have concluded to go to Greenville. Tell the folks there that I am coming in a few weeks.

I and grandma were talking while she was here and we concluded that you might as well leave some of your things in the attic there. You could leave the three heaviest comforts, the feather bed and pillows. I think Victor might leave his cot and the bed I made for it, also his carpet. By doing this you can pack everything else in your trunks. Papa will bring your trunk home with him on Thursday either in the morning or evening (evening I think). But you must have it ready for him if he should conclude to come in the morning. You can take his valise with you to Greenville as you do not intend to stay long. I want you to get fixed so that Victor can come home Fri. evening if possible and you must let us know on what train you will be home from Greenville so we can some of us meet you.

I hope you had a good time last Sat. night. I thought of you. Be sure to bring your oration home *[with]* you for I want to see it. I am expecting company for supper tonight.

Mon. 10 oclock

Well I had three preachers two preachers wives and two preachers daughters here for supper, have three of these folks here all night so I cant write much more. I am very tired and must be up early in the morning so I will say good by. Be sure you get all your things gathered up. Don't leave any thing behind for you know you are not at grandma's where you could go back after things.

Lovingly

Mamma

55. EFT in Lebanon to ELT in Salem, Saturday 14 July 1894

Dear Edith

I was up last night until just as the day light began to dawn and then Aunt Zie got up and took charge and I went to bed and then I overslept and did not get my letter written. Grandma is better and we hope she will soon be able to *[get]* up a little. The doctor says careful nursing is the thing he depends on for the most good. Just as soon as she wakes in the morning I light the little lamp stove and prepare a cup of tea or beef extract and she soaks a piece of the double baked bread in it and has a little nourishment right away.

Sunday morning *[July 15]*

Uncle Jem *[Flint]* came yesterday morning. The family in Decatur are all well. Myrtle *[Flint?]* is busy writing a book. The way she got the idea was amusing. I will tell you when I come home.

We have a visitor here for the last three days that has interested me not a little. It is a young girl a few months older than you. Her name is Mary Easterwood. She is from Clarence, Mo. She is very pretty and so gentle and grave I wondered at first why it could be that the child of such *[a]* roystering mother was so opposite, but after she told me something of her history I did not wonder. *[Edith Flint Thrall and Mary Eastwood were second cousins once removed.]*

She has been the patient nurse of her brother, mother, and two sisters all now dead and for four years has been speaking low and stepping softly for fear of disturbing the sick one. Just think, the years you have spent in college she has spent shut up amid pain and suffering. Her own health is failing and she is here trying to gather strength to go back and take *[care]* of her one remaining sister who they say cannot live till spring.

She is quite a fair musician and told me that sometimes in the summer evening when her mother and brother were so low she would play for them it seemed to soothe them. "By and by Willie would go to sleep & Mother would get so quiet" and some way she herself would seem rested.

Yesterday noon Uncle Will got word that Fred had been sold to the city marshall of Campsville, *[now Kampsville]* Calhoun Co. and Gerne's *[?]* team was sold to a mail carrier a little further on. The man who stole them is now in jail in Belleville. Uncle Will and Gerne with two officers went at five oclock Fri P.M. We have not heard anything from him yet. Uncle Henry brought from the city an enlarged copy of Mother's picture. It is very fine and she is so much pleased with it.

Etta Root came down to see me one evening last week. We talked some about rooms. Loudens *[Lowdens?]* have bought the Hobbs house. If mother keeps improving I will look around, and see what I can do.

Hobb's folks have bought the house that Kate had a room engaged in. I don't know what effect that will have on Kate's room.

Well Uncle Will is on his way home with old Fred. Will be here tonight. I think the old fellow will meet with quite an ovation. I have written a long letter but I missed getting one off yesterday. I will write to Papa tomorrow morning and will send no more now. Love to the boys. I am very hungry to get back home. The goods came all right. Do you think the grapes are ready? You are there though and know most about them.

I hope to be home in a few days at the outside.

Lovingly   Mamma.

56. EFT in Salem to ELT in Lebanon, 22 October 1894

Dear Edith

Your letter came all right and I was glad to hear from you. I do not know much about your trips to St. Louis and have never had them straight in my head yet. I am much better now although I still cough considerable.

I had a cold when I went to Muncie *[Indiana]* and the first house I went to they burned the natural gas without any stove pipes. A stove stood within two feet of my bed and a fire burned in it all night. It inflamed my lungs and Wed. night I had to go to a doctor. He relieved me but said I must not go back to the open stove. I thought then that I would have to go right home but Mrs. Hypes came to the rescue and took me home with her. I staid there until eight o clock Fri night.

A few minutes after nine that night we started home and traveled all night. I did not sleep any and took fresh cold so I got home pretty badly under the weather. Nelly was sick and I had to walk home from the depot. Papa was gone and oh dear there was so much to do and I was so poorly. I had not eaten as much as one good meal for four days and my appetite did not return for several days (I guess you folks at L. got it) so I am still weak. Have done no ironing for two weeks until today. Willie tried so hard to cook something I could eat and he got up some nice meals but you know how it is.

We had a very good session but I think it was hardly equal to the meeting held at Springfield two years ago. We only had two missionaries there Mrs. Forbes and Miss Carrol. There was a man "Olin Cady" on his way to Western China. He went about dressed in Chinese costume nearly all the time and made us a speech one night.

Madam Sorabji Cavalier the Persian lady who spoke at the Parliament of Religions at the world's fair *[in Chicago in 1893]* was there dressed in her native costume. She preached for us on Thursday night one of the sweetest most persuasive sermons I ever heard. "Christlike love the only sweetener of human relations." The next meeting of the Branch will be held at Eau Claire Wisconsin.

Muncie is a very pretty city of about 20,000 inhabitants. It is much cleaner than Metropolis. The streets look as if they were covered with smooth limestone slabs, sidewalks and streets just alike. In the homes there are neither wood coal dust or ashes. Natural gas is burned for everything.

The church is very beautiful. Dinner was served in the basement and we took breakfast and supper at our homes. After I moved I was in a nest of conf. secretaries and so got on to lots of business. I must tell you more of this when I see you. I want you to send me a piece of your new dress when you write again. I am glad you sent for it.

Bro. Wilkerson who was at Johnsonville *[Wayne County]* last year lost his wife last Thursday. Poor fellow he had not got moved. Now he is left with two little children. Mrs. Shultz's daughter Mrs. McFerrin died last Sat. morning and is to be buried today. Don't it seem hard for her Josie (the boy) and Lottie is all that now remains. Did you see the account of Carrie Gott's wedding? If I can do so conveniently I will send you a slip from the Central.

I feel very anxious about Grandma. I am glad Uncle Will is better. What about the Journal? Is there any chance for him to get it or is it a flash as so many things have been for him? Tell Uncle Fletcher I would be glad to hear from him and Aunt Gussie. I received Vickie's card today. Tell him Nellie *[a horse]* has spasmodic colic. She has not been hitched up yet since she got well.

Mrs. Martin is here with her baby. It looks so odd to see the old man walking about the yard with a tiny baby in his arms. I have a late letter from Aunt Carrie Campbell. All well. It is getting late and I am very tired. Love to Victor and Edith and don't forget yourself. Write as soon as you can.

Lovingly

Mamma

Has Robt. Young got well? You did say you had received the money in your last letter.

57. EFT in Salem to family, 19 November 1894

Dear children

Your letter came this noon. I will rise and explain in regard to last Fri night. Some two months ago our W.C.T.U *[Women's Christian Temperance Union]* proposed a prize contest. We hardly regarded it as a serious proposition until about three weeks ago when the matter took definite shape. I was one of the unhappy contestants and my companions were Mrs. Webster, Bryan, Leakin Merrill Burns and Bunton. I ought to had the prize of course but I did not get it. Mrs. Webster was the lucky one (not Grace Webster but her step mother-in-law). Of course we could not contend for a medal but there was a prize, a souvenir spoon called the Frances Willard spoon. It was a terrible night, cold, sleety, windy and dark but we had a good audience. Entrance fee a nickle for children, ten cents for adults. There were a great many complimentary admissions and then we took in nearly nine dollars. I shall have lots of fun telling you about it.

Papa was almost sick because he could not be there. He was at Sailors Springs *[Sailor Springs, Clay County, ten miles northeast of Flora]*. He said that there had not been anything in Salem before that he was so anxious to attend as that but his appointment had been made nearly two months and could not be changed.

The work on the district goes on a great deal better than the pay. Papa has paid the first insurance ($69.00) but had to borrow $10 from me and $40.00 from the missionary fund. He owes me over $50.00 now on my fifteen a week so you see I am greatly cramped. I think it very likely we will have to borrow money before next May but I think we will come out all right in the long run. Don't worry for we are not suffering.

Our missionary Society owes me over five dollars on my expenses to Muncie Ind. I have sent in my bill but have not heard from it. I have a cold at present but hope it will soon be better. So far I have usually made the fires. For the first week after I came home from Muncie I did not make fires. We keep a fire all night in the sitting room stove. We have scarcely any use at all for Nellie now and some times I wish we did not have her.

Papa and I drove over to Odin *[six miles west]* last Wednesday and spent the day with Bro. Littles folks. Mrs. L. sent love to you and Victor. Says she remembers you very well. The Thompson girls will probably not be home until after the "holidays."

About three weeks ago Bro. Thompson went down to the central part of Ky. And brought Mrs. T's aunt a very old lady to visit them. She intended to stay all winter but got homesick and went back a month ago this morning. Bro. T. had to go with her.

I had a letter from Uncle Willie last Sat. He seems very blue.

Your meetings don't seem to promise much. I am sorry but not surprised. Tomorrow night we have a "garment social" to be held at Y. S. Marshall's home. Admission one garment. You can bring as many as you want to spare so load up your spare duds and come. An order for a load of coal, a sack of flour or any other such trifle will be thankfully received.

We are needing rain very much. The wells around us are failing. Utterback's well runs out and then fills up. The parsonage well holds out well yet but three families are now drawing on it to some extent. There is some typhoid fever in town caused by low water. Little Fred Mitchell who used to live just south of us has had a long siege. He was thirty days without taking any solid food. He is getting well but is a shadow of a boy. Mrs. M. is very sick now. She tried to take care of him and do three or four washings a week beside. I am afraid she will die. I am glad your lecture course is opening so well.

Challis *[?]* cloth is selling for three to five cents per yard in town and it makes such pretty comforts but I can't *[?]* to buy some and make it up. I saw such a pretty one over Mrs. Martin's tonight. Have you any late news from Greenville? I have not.

We are going to have a Christmas treat or exhibition of some kind. Does your stove warm both rooms well? Is Vickie warm enough on his cot. I slept on ours last night and I felt too cool before morning. Then I thought of him. We are counting the days until Christmas for your visit.

We expect Edith to come with you.

Lovingly

Mamma

58. WFT in Salem to ELT, VWT, and Edith Gould in Lebanon, 2 December 1894

I will give you the same advice as Mrs. Seaman gave mamma about her letter and that is take the letter by serials!

Dear Sister—

It is Sunday afternoon and I thought I would make the dream you had the other night a reality. It is no wonder you dreamed that dream but I'll venture *[line faded]* your dream would become a reality. I am glad to hear that you are getting along nicely in college.

A little over a week ago Charlie and Willie Bullard took sick and mamma couldn't exactly tell what was the matter. It seemed to be a bad cold and trouble with the throat and lungs. Charlie was out of school all last week, but is about well now. Willie Bullard seems to be about the same as Charlie but Charlie got able to be out quicker than Willie B. This afternoon I saw Willie B. out on their porch. Last Friday Hallie took it and he is in the house all the time and in bed most of the time. He is very hoarse. I think he will be all right though in a few days.

I almost know you had a nice time Thursday at grandma's. We were going to have a chicken for dinner thanksgiving but Wednesday evening just as papa and I came home from a trip up town mamma came to the front of the house to see papa, staid and talked with him about 5 minutes while I was putting away the horse and buggy and when she again went into the kitchen she found on the table a huge, dressed turkey and a package of cranberries. We do not know where they came from. Brother Thompson got one at about the same time.

A week ago Friday afternoon I went with papa on one of his trips. We started Friday afternoon and drove to Patoka *[about 19 miles northwest]* then Saturday morning we went out to Mound Chapel 6 miles west of Patoka where the quarterly meeting was to be held. We staid there till Sunday afternoon when we drove to Sandoval, 15 or 16 miles and papa preached there Sunday night. In the morning early I drove home from Sandoval and left papa there. I got here just as the last bell for school was ringing and I had to put up the horse and do some chores about the house and then Charlie was sick so I did not go to school Monday morning. Papa preached in Odin Monday evening and came home on a late train. I had a real good time. I saw Jim Barnes who asked a good many questions about you.

Brother Little seems to be getting along nicely at Odin and Sandoval. That bad boy that he had was converted a week or so ago. Brother and Sister Little and one of their friends came over Wednesday and staid all day. We enjoyed their visit very much. (Wait a minute while I get Hally something. He is barking like a dog.) Hershel Hanckboner was in with some rabbits Wednesday eve. He staid all night and ate dinner Thursday. In the afternoon I went out with him and we went hunting but we didn't get but one rabbit (and the dogs caught that). I came home late Thursday evening.

Mamma and Charlie are at Sunday School. I stayed at home to tend to Hallie. Our Junior league held a pound social at poor old Mrs. MacElwain's house Thursday morning. The league swept up the house, made the beds, cooked her dinner, brought in her wood and other things. It was the second pound social we have had, the other one being at the house of our old lady named Goldsbury. We have over $8.00 in the treasury and we are going to have our organ. The president of our Junior League Mamie Farthing was to be in a medal contest last night but for some reason it did not come off.

I wish I could talk with you with my mouth. Monday we will get our grades for the month of November at school. Well did McKendree win Thursday at football?

(Sunday evening) Mamma and the children sent their love to you. There now you just step out of the room a while, I want to talk to Vic.

Your loving brother

W. F. Thrall

The Reverend Mister Victor Worthy Thrall DD. (Oh! Just anything to amuse the children.)

Dear Brother –

Well, I'm through ain't you glad. It's only 7.33 P.M. Sunday night Dec. 3rd 1894, so I have plenty of time although Mamma and Hallie have gone to bed. A little while ago I went to see Doctor Finley about Halley. He gave us some powders to give to him 3 times a day and a bottle with some medicine in it. We don't know just what it is but it has laudanum in it. The Doctor said that there were a good many similar cases in town.

Hardly had Freddie Mitchell got over the intermittent fever when his mother took seriously sick. Now she has recovered but her sister Mrs. Purcell and Noah her son have taken seriously sick with typhoid fever. At last reports Mrs. Purcell was no better but her boy was better. The Doctor will not allow Mrs. Mitchell to take care of her sister. Our washwoman Mrs. Asbury is also sick. Edith Asbury took the intermittent fever and it turned to typhoid. Mrs. Asbury sat up and watched with her all the time till now she is sick and for 2 or 3 weeks she has had someone else do the work. Three women have died within 24 hours. I can't name them all I don't think but I'll try, they were Jennie McQuin, Mrs. Dunlap and one more lady.

The poor of the town are in a destitute condition, speaking generally. Some of the families who are destitute are as follows: Hensley, Smith, Goldsbury, MacElwain, Sullens and a good many more. *[Will was a good reporter; this was the worst depression prior to the 1930s. See Jackson Lears, **Rebirth of a Nation**, 170f.]*

Miss Cellars, Carrie Brown's aunt is very sick. She probably will never be any better for we think it is consumption. I feel sorry for poor little Carrie. Mrs. Utterback told me to tell Carrie to come up Wednesday evening and get a chicken for their Thanksgiving dinner. She came but she came here first with a note from Miss Cellars. It was a pretty note, asking mamma whether to take the chicken or not and saying that she had never seen Mrs. Utterback but said that she thought she must be a very good woman and so on. Mamma told Carrie to take it of course and she went over after it. Mrs. Utterback had baked a cake for Thanksgiving but she said that it took so long for "Tom" and herself to eat a cake, so she put half of it into Carrie's basket. Carrie did not know it and when she lifted the basket she said that it must be a large chicken.

Well how are grandma and Uncle Willie and all of you getting along. If it won't bore you, I'll tell you something Dr. Finley said this evening. When I was there he asked me if papa was at home. I told him "no" and he said that he had intended to go to church for he thought papa was going to preach but he said that if he was not going to preach it would not be worth while to walk clear up to the church.

Our Epworth league is doing a great deal of work among the poor. They had a garment social at Mrs. Marshall's the other night and the admission fee was one garment of some sort. They are being distributed among the poor of the town.

My but you must be awfully tired by this time, I sympathize with you. Nellie does not seem to get along very well. Since she was so sick she has took to cribbing and she eats up nearly every thing around. She is now eating up a place in the fence I guess so she can get out. I got some salt rock but it does not seem to do much good. I want you to hurry up and come and see what is the matter with her. I am sorry to have to tell you this but I think she will get all right soon.

Tom has been sick but is convalescing (to save you the trouble of referring to Webster I will tell you what that means. It means "getting better," I think.) Charlie's new cat by name Belshazzar has to be watched or it will kill itself by eating too much. Beelzebub (Tom) plays with it a great deal and amuses the children. We also call Tom "the Doctor."

We boys at school have organized a football eleven. We had a nice football but one of the No. 8 boys put a nail in his shoe and kicked it and put a hole in it. We had to send it to the shoemaker to fix it but it wasn't done in time to play our game set for Thanksgiving afternoon. We did not have any school from Wednesday the rest of last week. I am getting along pretty well in school but have been out several times on account of being sick.

My pencil is getting dull so I guess I will close pretty soon for tonight. I hope we will hear from you in the morning. We have been getting up miserably late here of late. Yesterday we did not have breakfast till about 9.30 A.M. I'm going to quit for they've shut me out in the cold so I won't bother them in there. Well I guess I'll rest for the night. Good-night, then.

Monday morning – Well I guess I did not tell you that I had a sore mouth. It had been bothering me for some time but it was not very serious but this morning I woke up and found that the whole roof of my mouth was inflamed. I can't bear to have anything but bread and milk touch it not even my tongue so I can't sound all sounds and therefore I cant talk plain. I guess I won't go to school this morning on that account.

Hallie and I are in bed here in the sitting-room. Hallie is some better this morning. He has some fever. He is on the bed here by my side playing with that stuffed cat.

Charlie has just returned from the post-office. He bought a package of stamped envelopes. He said that there was a letter in the box but he forgot to get it. We have not heard from the mail since Saturday morning. We expect papa this afternoon. He went to Cisne and Johnstonville *[probably Johnsonville, six miles west of Cisne in Wayne County]* this last trip.

You remember I. G. Morrill of course. Well papa gets a letter from him every once in a while. He lives at St. Elmo now. Not long ago papa got a letter from him asking papa this: "If I can get a wife who will be a good help to me can you give me a place as supply at some charge." Papa answered it and I don't know exactly what he did tell him. I know he did not give him a charge though.

O. B. Ray who kept the news stand sold out to Mrs. Belle Johnston and Clarence Chance and he and his brother invented a patent olive *[?]* blacking. Then they kept a billiard hall, then a pool-room and lastly they have set up a grocery store.

I heard "Billy" Bryan of Nebraska speak here Thursday night at the court house on the subject of "Money" advocating free silver bimetalism and nearly everything else. *[William Jennings Bryan was later a three-time candidate for the Presidency; his father attended McKendree.]*

Tell Edith that her card came Saturday. We got a card from papa stating the he would send you that money he had forgotten to give me the check.

I am up now and dressed. It is after 11oclock so I must hasten. I suppose you know all about Charlie Bauchens. At any rate I will tell now. About a month ago he was in O'Fallon learning the art of telegraphy. Well I was at the Royal Templars of Temperance *[page torn]* when I heard that a barrel of lime had fallen on his leg and that the bone had been crushed above the knee. Well the next day the truth about it came out. The barrel of lime fell on his leg making a clean break below the knee. He has not been out yet but is getting better very slowly. Mrs. A. R. Bryan is seriously sick and is not expected to live long. Well I guess I had better close, you please step out and admit your venerable cousin.

Your loving brother

W. F. Thrall

Dear Cousin Edith *[Edith Gould, daughter of Leonidas's sister Laura (Thrall) Gould]*—I thought I would have to tell you to write to us and tell us all about yourself. How do you get along in college. I suppose you like it very well. You must write to us for those other people in the same house with you never even mention you. Tell us about the folks at Bone Gap. Tell us all about Cousin Virgil's baby especially *[probably Edward Malcolm Gould, son of Edith Gould's brother Virgil]*. What was his first words? How much does he weigh? When did he cut his first tooth? What is his politics? Has he any decided religious inclinations? What is the young man's name? Did your fruit get there all safe or was it frozen?

Remember what I say be sure and write to us. I am longing for Christmas time to see you. Say by the way you might bring those other people there in the same house with you. We'll make room for them. Hoping your success I remain as ever your

Loving Cousin

W. F. Thrall

(to one and all)

"and now I'm through this weary work, From reading it pray do not shirk." (Original) (Good-bye.)

59. EFT in Salem to ELT 28 February 1895

Dear Edith

We are all tolerable well this morning. Willie has been poorly with an obstinate kind of bowel trouble, but was able to go to school this morning. Yesterday and the day before was the grand council of R. Y of Y. They had the supreme Councilor of the world here too. They had a rather stormy session, boxed Y.S.M.'s ears right and left for not working up the order in the state but they selected him Grand Councilor of the state. I rather think the order is declining especially the insurance part.

I am going to write to Vickie soon. Col Dickie lectured here last Tues. evening in the M. E. church. A very fine lecture.

We were at Mary Nelms wedding last Tues. afternoon. She will live at Grand Crossing Ill. *[probably Chicago]* Papa got five dollars for the job. Mr. Mulford of Greenville (Tommie's papa) committed suicide a week ago last Sunday. I am going to a tea-party this evening given by the C.P. *[probably Cumberland Presbyterian]* Missionary Society. I don't know where it is. I go as Mrs. Webster's guest and she comes for me in her Surrey at four oclock.

An evangelist is to come here on the eighth of next month and hold a union meeting. The man is a C. P. He has a brother who is a Methodist but he is out of fix just now. I send you five dollars in this letter. I hope to be able to send you ten next week. Is Victor needing the money he loaned me for grandma?

Things begin to look a little like spring here. Two or three persons have spoken to me about your quartette! I did not pay much attention to them but I will be more careful in the future. I should not wonder if you could work up a chance here.

You would better send in that application. They ask if you insist on a certain locality. I hardly think that would be wise but I think I would express a preference. I think you could do that. I do not see my way clear to set a time to come to Lebanon at present. I may possibly come but it is likely will not be there until June.

Lovingly

Mamma

60. EFT's brother William Winterton Flint in Lebanon to ELT in Salem 18 March 1895

Dear Edith

Mother *[Mary (Gedney) Flint]* wants me write to you to tell you that she wants some of that medicine. When you write to your Uncle Jim *[Flint]* tell him to send some medicine for her too. When he sends us anything he usually sends it to Fletcher *[Flint]* in St. Louis to save express. I suppose he will do this the same. Mother also says to tell you not to forget to tell your mother what she told you to tell her.

We received a letter Saturday from your Uncle Wesley *[Rev. John Wesley Flint]* telling of Minnie's serious illness. He said Zie had not been to bed since last Saturday and he not since Tuesday. The doctor pronounced it Grip-pneumonia and said that she might recover but it would tax every ounce of strength and require careful watching both day and night. Friday morning the symptoms were favorable. We have heard nothing since and hope that no news is good news. Have you any late word from there—if so write us.

I feel just like I was taking the grip myself tonight. Mother is very poorly tonight and has been for several days. Just now she either has a bad cold or is taking the grip. I hope your mother is better than when she wrote us last Friday night. Of course the pleasurable surprise you gave her Saturday morning was a good tonic.

Charlie *[Will W. Flint's son]* sends his love to Vickie & Edie. He also sends a hug and kiss to each of them—the first one for Vick. and the second for Edie. Mr. Peach seems about the same. Mr. Sager & Charlie Wise are better. Carrie has gone to the Commencement of the commercial class tonight. The lecture Saturday night was very good I'm told. Prof. Brownlee was in town today. Henry was out, and reported everything "about the same." Fletcher has been poorly for a week—but still attending to business. No late word from Mary, Jim, or George.

No news. Election is all the go just now.

Love to All

Write. Will W. Flint

61. EFT to ELT in Salem 30 April 1895

Dear Edith

Your letter reached me yesterday morning and Victor read it to me while I was cooking dinner for a household of company. It was brought into the parlor and disappeared from mortal view so I have never had my hands on it. I hope to find it sometime.

Some of the changes in the faculty surprised us a little but I guess it is all right. The boys had a fine success in their concert—but I guess the league is out of pocket a little. There is quite a strong feeling in favor of their return but I don't know how it will turn out.

Papa went to Effingham this morning to preach bro Lecavits funeral. He died Sun. A.M. while papa was holding his Q. M. *[Quarterly Meeting]*. Papa is not very well. The death and the extra work it involves and the district conf. all coming together seem to be a little too much for him. Bro. Kimball assistant preacher at Eff. *[Effingham?]* has taken charge of Montrose Ct. *[circuit?]*

In regard to that toast business I am busy but will try and do something. I believe as you give me choice of subject I will say write me down for "The Girls." I shall divide them into two classes. The old girls of which I am one and the new girls of which you and Kate are one.

I have bought me a new silk waist and shall not buy a new dress until after com. Victor and I are going out in the country a while this evening. He says be sure and send out his laundry if you have not already done so. Goodby

Mamma.

62. EFT in Salem to ELT and VWT in Lebanon 23 May 1895

Dear Edith and Victor

Your letters came all right and we were so glad to hear from you. No other letter ever comes into the house that meets so warm a welcome as yours do.

I am alone in the house today. Papa and Willie are in Centralia at the League convention. Charlie and Harold are out riding. Everything is so still. I look for the folks home tonight. I wrote my paper and sent it by papa. It did not seem possible for me to go, and I am glad I did not try.

Mrs. Utterback went to Springfield a week ago last Monday. I think she will be back next Fri. I don't know whether she will still be here when you come back or not. If you boys go to Sandoval you must let us know a few days before. I am glad that you made a dollar a piece. That is better than nothing. I don't know who paid the deficiency here. It was never brought before the League.

A letter from Aunt Lizzie *[Leonidas's older sister Mary Elizabeth (Thrall) Morgan]* today spoke of Aunt Laura's *[Laura Lucina (Thrall) Gould]* recent sickness but said she was better. Cretia *[Mary Elizabeth's daughter]* came near losing her baby a short time ago but it is better now.

Old man Hull is near death with tobacco tremens. I had a talk with Blanch last Sunday. She cannot be at commencement. Her mother-in-law is likely to die any hour and she is with them so you see it is impossible for her to come. She asked me if Sadie Foster was going to respond to a toast—and if so what? Aunt Carries toast is "Clio."

I send you in this letter twenty one dollars. I don't expect this to cover your expenses home. I shall bring money for that and if you need more don't be afraid to say so and will do the best I can. I don't need to spend much more for myself and the children before we come. Charlie and Harold need hats and one more new waist apiece. Mattie Knight will sew for me next Sat.

I have nothing new to say in regard to papa except a general listlessness that creeps over him. I am counting a great deal on the inspiration that you children will bring to him. I have written to Uncle Will. Love to all

Write soon

Lovingly

Mamma

Willie has a job berry picking next week.

63. EFT in Lebanon to ELT 28 July 1895

Dear Edith

I will write to you today for I know I have been neglecting you. I guess you are busy and have not had much time to write. Grandma and Uncle Will are both very poorly especially Uncle. I think I never saw him so feeble. Carrie and Charlie are in East St. Louis; have been gone since last Wed. and will be home tomorrow night.

I have put up ten quarts of fruit for Vickie. I am going to Jepsons tomorrow night to buy that curtain. Jessie came down an evening last week and brought you a photo of herself. Uncle Fletcher called on his way home from church and said that Charlie Andrews had preached a very fine sermon this morning.

I have not heard a word from Kate nor have I seen anything of her. Have you anything late in regard to her visit? I am getting anxious to get home again and expect to be there on the date I wrote to Harold. Is Anna still with you? Thank her for my belt pin.

Uncle Will talks of going to Decatur in a week or two for a visit of a week or more. I do hope he be able to go and get some good from the trip. Ed. McDonald a cousin of Cretie [?] Herron died in St. Louis yesterday and his body passed the house a short time ago. It will be buried here tomorrow. I suppose his name was mentioned in that Clio invitation you sent to one of the McDonald girls last May and had it returned to you from the dead letter office.

I have finished Mother's new dress and made over her pink one and made her two new gowns. I have not gone out very much nor seen many people since I came here. Mr. Spragg told me at League last Sunday night that he looked at me a long time during church in the morning trying to remember who I was (I was not at church). The Lewis girls are going to Piasa Bluffs next Thursday for a week. I think we will have a rain tonight it is looking very stormy at this time 2 P.M. Hope you are having a pleasant Sunday.

Lovingly

Mamma

64. Samuel Fletcher Flint in Lebanon to EFT 23 December 1895

Dear Sister

I cant write a letter today, but I want to drop a word in your ear. We want to get a reclining chair for *[brother]* Will; he cant rest in any chair we have, & one like he so needs will *[cost]* $10.00 or $12.00. Please let us know as soon as you can how much can *[put]* toward it. I will do my part, but cant buy it alone.

Will is very weak, but no worse than when Vick went home.

With love

Fletcher

[Edith's youngest brother, William Winterton Flint, died 25 January 1896]

65. Annie E. Kirkland Flint (wife of EFT's brother George) in Waggoner to EFT 16 April 1896

Sister Edith:

Forgive me for such neglect but believe me I have not written a line to any one but Father since leaving L. *[Lebanon]* We learned of your move to Lebanon through the Central. You are now so near college I know it will be a pleasure to you—sorry to learn you and Lonnie are not well. You did not mention Edith is she home?

We have been so busy for nearly two months that we have had little time for anything but work. George has not had an idle day since we commenced to move. We have all been well—through Earl *[their son]* complains sometimes with his old head ache attacks. Think he will outgrow them soon. He could not get interested in the school here so we allowed him to remain out as the school closes with this month and he would not lose much. He is quite a help to George at times.

We have a small house here but the kitchen is the largest we have had since leaving our old Greenville home. We have some garden and potatoes in and George finished putting in twelve acres of oats to-day so if the season is favorable will have something coming in after while. I feel so much encouraged since coming here for I know that with good health we can make a living and I hope something more.

Louise *[their daughter]* is a little rowdy. I made her a sunbonnet and she is never happier than when outside chasing around[.] she is much more mischeifous than Earl and a little rattler to talk. In one of your letters you inquired about her picture. I had only a few taken and expected to send one or two to friend in exchange. May send you one yet.

Is Carrie with Mother Flint now? I owe her a letter and hope to write soon—It makes me sad to think of Willie being gone. Of course you are aware of the many deaths there have been in Greenville the past year. We still have a paper from there still feel more attachment for there than any other place.

Earl and I must go plant some beans and it will then be supper time.

Hope you can read this scrawling.

Earl will write Hallie soon. My love to Mother Flint and all the relatives.

We are always glad to hear from you.

Ann E.

66. EFT in Lebanon to LWT 29 April 1896

Dear Lonnie

Your letter came today. I am glad you are feeling well, and I guess you are a long way on your road. This has been a cloudy day. I am better. I have not taken any medicine (except Dr. Fikes) today or yesterday. I was very tired when I got the work done after dinner today and lay down and went to sleep. Have not had much fever this week.

Edith went to Belleville this A.M. to attend the Dist. association of the W. F. M. S. *[Women's Foreign Missionary Society]* She will be home tomorrow night. A letter came from Bro. Kimball with $11.00 in it. After reading the letter over carefully twice I have concluded to send it to you. You know how much allowance to make for the personality of the writer and it is likely you have heard something of the matter under discussion since I saw you.

A letter came from Bro. Gooch announcing his safe arrival in Patoka. He with his family are at Squire Farmer's and he filled the Sunday's appointments and seemed much pleased. His furniture had not come when he wrote. He asked when his quarterly meeting was so I told him on a card. I send you in this letter also one from Bro. Reeves. These three letters are all that have come and I have waited for today's mail.

Victor has been suffering very much with toothache. Was real sick Monday night. He is better now but he had to go to the dentist and have his tooth treated. We begin to miss you in earnest for this is the time you usually get home. I do hope you will stand the journey well. You will have lots of company on the way I guess.

There has been no news in town since you left. I did not go to church Sunday. It was raining and I was not well. I think I will buy Charlie's suit this week so he can go to church. Mother came down yesterday morning and will stay till tomorrow night at least. We hope to hear from you soon.

Lovingly

Edith

67. EFT in Lebanon to LWT 3 May 1896

Dear Lonnie

Your letter came this morning but the paper has not come. I think you have missed the first letter I wrote. I told you in that letter about receiving the Louisville money and also sent you Bro. Kimball's letter. I directed the same way that the other letters were directed.

Victor had a hard chill this noon. The fever is just going down. I have some quinine and will try to ward off the next one. He has been real sick all day, and of course could not go to church.
Edith leads the league tonight. Her thesis is done and I am foolish enough to think that it is a remarkably able paper. We were very much interested in your account of the work Fri. You told us some things that we did not get in the paper. Today our news boy left us without a paper.

It is growing dark so goodbye dear *Have a good time*

Lovingly

Edith

68. EFT in Lebanon to LWT at Hawley House, Cleveland, Ohio, Monday 5 May 1896

Dear Lonnie

Your good letter reached us this morning. We were sorry to know that you had been feeling poorly, and hope you are better now. I have been feeling quite well for me until today. I have aching in my right lung. I am using the iodine again. I felt well only that ugly ache.

Victor has been real sick all day. Is loaded up with quinine and I have sat by the lounge here in the sitting room nearly all day with him. He looks very bad but we hope the chill will not come tomorrow and then he will begin to mend.

The Daily Advocate came this morning. Many thanks for it and the papers you mean to send too. Work on the college progressing finely so far as I know. I received a letter from Bro D. Orr this afternoon with eleven dollars and fifty cents in it. He reports a *good* quarterly meeting and general prosperity. They paid Bro Gilham $1.00 expenses. Have not heard from the other quarterly meeting but it is very early yet, you know.

As for that committee business—well broadcloth will not always cover bristles. I hope you will enjoy your work and I know you will do faithful work. We think of you so often and pray for you every morning. I hope you will get some letters soon. This is the fifth one I have written.

Goodnight,

Lovingly

Edith

69. CHT in Lebanon to LWT in Cleveland, Ohio, probably 6 May 1896

Dear Papa:

I have read all of your letter with interest. Did they vote on the woman question to-day? If so how did it come out? I hope the women will get their rights. I have a new suit and shoes and stockings. My suit is a brownish gray. Hoping success to you in all your *[illegible]*, I will close.

Charlie Thrall

70. EFT in Lebanon to LWT at Hawley House, Cleveland, Ohio, 8 May 1896

Dear Lonnie

This A.M. I received a letter from *[you]* and tonight another. The Daily of May 5 came also. We are all pretty well at present and glad to hear that you are better. I noticed *[in]* the Daily received today that they are going to paint the glass roof of the armory. I guess that will help matters some. I should think it would be dreadfully warm in there with the sun shining on you. Do you have good food where you are?

There is absolutely no news here. The Baptists had a lawn social and ice cream supper last night in the grounds around their church and as it grew late and the better class of people began to go home the toughs gathered and they made night hideous until nearly midnight.

Victor has been busy practicing a song "Robin Adair" for a musical to be given by Prof Johnston in about ten days or two weeks. It is very pretty.

Carrie [?] has been having trouble with one of her eyes. It has been inflamed since Sunday and don't seem to get better. They are getting along real well with the old house.

We have read the speeches on the women question with great interest. I guess your idea of the finding at the last is about correct.

I must send this to the mail now.

Lovingly

Edith

71. EFT in Lebanon to LWT, "Wednesday A.M.," possibly 13 May 1896

Dear Lonnie

We are well as usual this morning. Dr. W. examined Charlie's chin yesterday afternoon and said it needed another burning plaster and so he put one on. Yesterday I heard from the two quarterly meetings.

Bro. Harris sent me $7.97. Bro. Wallar's [?] expenses were $2.28. The deficiency was $1.75. Kinmundy reported $8.85. Bro. Nall's expenses 1.15. Deficiency was 2.00.

This morning Willie will pay his tuition. I found Mother needing money badly and paid her $2.00. I expect to pay her the rest next week. She did not ask for it but she seemed very glad to get it. I am using my money just as carefully as possible. I shall have to pay Victor's building and loan out of this week's income.

It was thundering at daylight this morning but it does not now look like rain. I think a big rain would wash your lime and mud into streaks and give you clouds and sunshine both, all the time.

The coincidence in regard to your text and that of Bro. Mains was singular to say the least. Carrie says "I bet Lonnie preached the best sermon." Do you think Bro. Chamberlain will find anyone to help him on the million for McKendree while at general conference? I should be very glad to know that he had.

I must tell you Ediths dream last Sat. night. She dreamed we had all died and were in heaven and you was a presiding elder there just the same as here. Well I would better quit now. We have received no dailies this week.

Lovingly

Edith

72. EFT in Lebanon to LWT at Hawley House, Cleveland, Ohio, 6 A.M. 15 May 1896

Dear Lonnie

I did so enjoy your letter yesterday.

We are well as usual. I am not taking any medicine now though I still use the iodine. It is very cool this morning. So cool in fact that I think I will take my writing into the kitchen. The sun is shining brightly and it will soon be warm.

I was so sorry to hear the bad news from Crete *Britton [Lucretia (Morgan) Britton, daughter of Leonidas's older sister Mary Elizabeth (Thrall) Morgan]* and do sincerely hope she is better before now.

I saw in the paper last night the action of the general conference in regard to Bishops Bowman and Foster. I think that is right but I did not like the motion to arbitrarily retire them. Some way it seemed to me there was no Christlike tenderness in it though there might be "financial ability" displayed in the first thought; but "there is that withholdeth more than is mete and it tendeth to poverty." In regard to this matter of course I talk from newspaper reports and may be inaccurate. I would have enjoyed Amanda Smith's singing I know I would like to see her. I think she must be a power.

We had heard something about the little breeze in regard Y. P. S. C. E. It seems there are some men in the conference who grow excited over trifles. You know when a vessel is full it runs over whether it holds a hogshead or a gill.

The ladies did well with their ice cream social. They made over seventeen dollars the rainy night and then sold again last night after prayer meeting.

The ladies of the M.E. church in Salem gave the banquet to the High School Alumni this month. I guess Aunt Harriet Marshall had a good time. I think Victor intends to write some to you this morning. So goodbye

Lovingly

Edith

8 A.M. Have just read the report in Globe which says that they did retire Bowman and Foster. Well may be I am too far away to judge.

73. EFT in Lebanon to LWT at Hawley House, Cleveland, Ohio, 16 May 1896

Dear Lonnie

It rained a great deal in the night and is now raining not very hard but a steady businesslike down pour. The rain we have had this week has been of great service to the farmers. We are all well today.

The last of that trouble came away from Charlie's yesterday. The sore is not yet quite well but I think a few days will heal it. I went up on College Hill yesterday. Went with Edith to Clio. The girls had a good program and were as a rule well prepared. Then later Edith and Willie and myself went up and listened to Philo's program for half an hour then went over and listened to Plato's debate. Neither of the boy's societies had a very full attendance. Hallie had part in the program at school Hall last night and does again tonight.

I wrote you Wednesday an account of the finances from the last two quarterly meetings. I think the people on the district have done real well. The first deficiencies were reported last week and were not very large. We are getting along very well. I hope to get the money from Salem and Alma all right and this will help us a great deal.

Our garden looks very pretty. I am late this morning and must close. You will be with us again in less than two weeks. We are all looking forward with pleasure to the time.

Lovingly

Edith

74. EFT in Lebanon to LWT at Hawley House, Cleveland, Ohio, 17 May 1896

Dear Lonnie

This is Sunday morning. We had another rain last night.

Edith went down to stay all night at Mother's. Carrie wanted to spend the night with a Mrs. Pfeffer whose husband is out of town. Victor went to St. Jacobs last night. The quartet were invited to sing at an entertainment. They went in a surrey and came back after the entertainment. He reported a good performance after he got home. Their expenses were paid. Harold had a part in the school exhibition and Charlie went with him. So Willie and me spent the evening here. He was writing out a lot of Latin sentences for Prof. Baker.

I have not heard anything from Wayne City. There have been no letters come for you save a bid from a marble firm in Centralia for monuments for Bros Thomson and Douthilt *[quite possibly J. B. Thompson who died 1896 in Salem and C. T. Douthit who died 1896 in Patoka]*. They wished you to call at once and see their work before buying elsewhere.

How are things progressing with you now? You seem to be having a struggling time over the election of Bishops. It looks as if McCabe might be elected unless there is a landslide.

Well I hope the best side will gain. Did you get to shake hands with Mr. Kinsley? Or did n't you want to? [*Could this be 1896 presidential nominee and Ohioan William McKinley?*] We received two dailies yesterday. Tomorrow I will try and send you a complete list of all we have. I am glad you did not preach today. It seems to me you ought to have a little rest from preaching so much and then it may be refreshing to hear some of the others preach a few times.

The college buildings look very fresh and nice. Commencement visitors are coming in already. Mostly old students.

I received a Greenville Advocate which brought news that Seaman voted against the billiard hall. Did you get that letter in time to write to him? I hope you will have a pleasant Sunday.

Lovingly

Edith

Maybe you would better pay that ten dollars to Chamberlain. Dont send it here. We have a bill at the store but hope to pay some on it this week.

75. EFT in Lebanon to LWT at Hawley House, Cleveland, Ohio, 18 May 1896

Dear Lonnie

I write some what hurriedly this morning. We are well as usual.

Bro. Powers preached last night on "Ingersol's bible." [*Robert G. Ingersoll, the "Great Agnostic" speaker and writer*] I attended the League services but did not stay to church. This morning looks a little gloomy. Not rainy at all but the clouds are low and heavy. I have been so busy I have not read as much of the dailies as I would have liked but I still hope to read them all.

Victor's work is growing lighter. He will soon be through with two of his five studies. The other three will hold on until the close of the term.

The public schools will close with their annual picnic next Friday. I expect to take Harold with me to Salem tomorrow and so he will miss the picnic but nothing of school work that will have any bearing on his promotion. His examinations are all over and his teacher told me it would make no difference for him to be away the days following the handing in of his papers.

I think we will have very little fruit here. The cherries have about all fallen off and there were very few pear blossoms. Do you have plenty of strawberries? We don't see many here. I bought two quarts one day and they were very inferior and cost fifteen cents per qt. I did not feel like investing any more money in them.

Send my letters to Salem in care of [?] Utterback. I had a letter from her yesterday but did not hear from you. I shall go to Salem tomorrow and come home on Fri. That is my present plan.
Write to the children here. This will impose two letters a day on you for a little while. Do you see anything more of Amanda Smith? Is Lucy Rider Meyer there? I cannot keep track of all the reports or resolutions offered to the G.C. *[General Conference]* I suppose many die in the committee rooms.

Lovingly Goodbye

Edith

76. ELT to LWT in Cleveland 20 May 1896

Lebanon, Ill May 20 – 1896

Dear Papa:

I believe mamma either took our tablet with her or hid it for it hasn't been seen since she left. So I will have to write on this old scrap of exam. paper for it's all I can find. Mamma got off yesterday morning at 8.23. It was thundering & blowing & rained nearly all the morning although it cleared up long enough for us to drive her to the depot.

Victor I think is feeling all right again. The rest of us here are well as usual. I got hold of a Post Dispatch *[St. Louis daily newspaper]* and read the news from the elections. I think you have had quite a time voting on those bishops. And McCabe & Cranston finally got there. I know there must have been a wild scene when the election was announced. I did so enjoy your letter about the Epworth League rally. It made me wish more than I ever had that I could have been there. I tried to persuade mamma to stay over Sun. in Salem to hear Bro Young preach and make her visit a little fuller. I rather think she will although she wouldn't say.

Mrs. Chamberlain & Wilson were in last night. Mrs. Chamberlain said Mr. C. would probably be home Sat. or Mon. & Clifford possibly sooner. I know they must be anxious to see the buildings since they have been painted for they are so pretty. Are you folks having much rain in Cleveland. I'll tell you we are getting plenty here. Had another big one last night.

We are getting so hungry to see you again and it's only a week & a day. I hope this difficulty in electing Bishops wont delay you. You just must have time to stay with us & rest some before you go to Patoka for the next week is Conv. you know and we will have no chance to visit then. I have got to write to mama now so I will close. We will have to all of us write twice a day for a while now, wont we. We rec'd no Advocates yesterday.

Lovingly

Edith

77. EFT in Salem to WFT in Lebanon, 22 May 1896
Salem III.

Fri. May 22. /96

Dear Willie

Edith's letter came last night. I do hope you have received that letter from Burkitt with the money. I have not received any more here. I am getting anxious to get home. I shall do some of my trading today. Perhaps all of it. I only see Harold now and then. I am at Mrs. Utterback just now. I took supper at Thompsons last night. Grace looks very bad. The rest seem all right.

The convention is over and gone. For many things it was fine but some things about it did not suit me entirely. Prof Fager is the district president. Edith failed to send that railroad letter. Maybe I will get it today. I wonder if Victor has seen Etta. *[illegible]* will not teach next year.

I must close now but will not post this until afternoon I may find something I want to add to it.

Lovingly

Mamma

I think Etta could get $50. or more per month. That railroad letter has not come.

78. ELT to LWT in Cleveland 22 May 1896

Lebanon Ill. May 22 -96

Dear Papa:

Your little letter received and I have done just the same trick you did—have overslept and it is now 8.15. So about all I have time to say is that we are well and it is raining. We have had so much rain lately—nearly every day. We will be so glad when you get home. It has been such a long time.

Lovingly

Edith

79. EFT in Salem to LWT in Cleveland 23 May 1896

Salem Ill. Sat. May 23. 1896.

Dear Lonnie

We were so glad to hear from you yesterday. It seems so good to think that you are well and able to work as you want to and not be exhausted. I am feeling well and everyone says I am looking so well. I was with Sister Davenport for supper last night and had a very pleasant visit.

Bro Young called in after supper. He seems well and well satisfied. They tell me good things about him. They say he has good things to say and knows when to quit. That you know is very desirable in a preacher.

I walked up to the post office from the church with Bro. Kimball Thursday afternoon. He said in a very matter of fact way "Bro. Thrall will have a very easy time at conference next time. None of the leading charges will want to change and appointments of other grade are so easily managed." I thought he was trying to find out if he could if any important changes were to come. The talk here is "no change."

I went into Bessie's millinery store yesterday to look at some hats for Edith and myself and found them in a state of excitement over the report that a baby had just died on the counter in White's store. Someone went over to see and the story was true.

I have as yet only received ten dollars from Salem but Bro Wilson said he would have it all before I went home. I told Bro Burkitt to send his money straight to Edith but she had not got it early yesterday morning. He said he had it raised. I hope she got it yesterday for I know she needed it.

Neither Bro Borah nor Bro Loar were at the convention, neither were Bros. Alexander, Vandeveer, Galbreath, Perrin, Little nor Scanthon and but one Baker, the one from Xenia. Still I think there was a good representation. Bro. K. preached for Bro Van Cleve at Mt. Vernon last Sunday and he seemed perfectly carried away with the place and the people. Bro Van Cleve would better look out a little I think. Gen. Martin is in poor health.

Well good by dear I hope you will have a good Sunday. I go home on the early train Monday. I have bought some matting for Edie's room.

Lovingly

Edith

80. EFT in Lebanon to CHT in Salem 20 July 1896

Lebanon Ill Mon. July 20, 1896.

Dear Charlie

Your letter came last Sat. night. I was glad to hear from you. We are tolerably well. I am taking medicine from Dr. Wagoner and he thinks I will be right well again soon. A letter from Papa this morning reports him well. How is Charlie Young? And how is Mrs. Marshall? Find out and tell me when you write again. When is my Sunday School class coming to see me? Send word how the Junior League is prospering and other things too.

Harold has started out as an agent for the Ram's Horn and has cleared $1.25 since Sat. noon. Has the money in his pocket. He hopes to double it before the week is out. Ask Mrs. Anthony to show you her Ram's Horn of July 18 and look on the second page. Well I will just cut out the "Special Offer" and send it to you. If you think you want to try it in Salem all right. Harry is jubilant over his success.

We have had a tremendous rain since last night. Kate went home this morning. They sent for her.

Love to all the folks, write soon.

Lovingly,

Mamma

81. EFT in Lebanon to LWT in Cisne 3 June 1897, "care of Rev. J. M. Mulvaney" on stationery of the Vandalia District Advocate Monthly, "L.W. Thrall, Editor, Lebanon, Ill."

Lebanon, Illinois, June 3 1897

Dear Lonnie

I received your letter containing order for twelve dollars last Monday evening. Many thanks for both. I sent you a letter to Kinmundy containing some mail that I thought you ought to have. There came a card from L. J. *[?]* Boyer day before yesterday saying he would hold your quarterly meeting and asking you to write to him and tell him the way to go or have Bro. Fisk do so. I was not certain just when the meeting was and wrote to Fisk at once to send him a letter of direction. Then a little later I found a copy of the District Advocate and in it the date of the Q.M.

There is here a list of names sent from Y. A. Eaton planning for the distribution of 94 Advocates containing his sermon also a brief letter containing $2.30 to pay for said copies. I have two or three unexpected calls for small sums of money and if I should need that money I suppose it would be all right to use it. I am not needing it now but may possibly do so before you get home. I thought of you at the convention many times during its session and hoped you was still feeling well and able to enjoy it.
Victor had a letter from Bro. Gooch Saturday saying that he had been obliged to go to Kentucky again but expected to be in the house by commencement but we have not seen any of him this week so far.

Many visitors are already in town. J. A. Sarge and G. E. McCammon are here. Ada Otwell came Tuesday evening and Josie last night. Charlie has two of his grades already—96 in each. Mrs. Root was called to Johnsonville to a very sick child of May Blake's. The child was better last night.

We had a fine rain last night. It is a little after six and no one is up but me but I hear a stirring among the dry bones up stairs. I hope you are sleeping this morning. We all love you, think of you, pray for you. I hope to hear again today.

Lovingly Edith

We have been unable to find that card of Bro. Kimballs. Will has not got it. If we do find it I will preserve it. I am so glad that the fund is assured for your trip. If I am able to go I know we will see a good time.

82. Annie E. (Kirkland) Flint in Raymond to EFT in Lebanon, 18 June 1897

Rarymond, Ill. June 18th 97

Dear Sister Edith:

I can scarcely believe that three Sabbaths have almost past since receipt of your letter—but as it lies before me in plain black it must be so—it certainly was a welcome surprise to hear from you—I am so negligent cannot remember when I wrote last—Am glad to know you are all on the mend. I first heard of Mr Thralls illness through the Central. We were then at sister Libbie's and packed ready to come here we had to remain there a week before the roads were passable—I thought at the time I surely would write—but so many things to worry us caused it to be postponed—Well I am glad he had strength to conquer and hope the trouble with the ear has left by this time—You once wrote that Charlie was not well at all but I did not understand in what way he was affected. I congratulate him on his happy solution of the trouble.
We are all in good health and tanned as most farmers are—The Children seem to like it here. There is only one boy in the near neighborhood and he and Earl are to-gether often. We have kind neighbors. I went to sister Libbie's last week my first trip since coming here. It is between 7 and 8 miles to their place—We are 2 ½ miles from town. I have not been there so you see I don't gad about much

Of course there is plenty work to keep one busy and the season has been so late that we have little to show for all we have done—Friday George finished planting corn 40 acres—but of course that is all in the future. Last year he had the same when the floods came and destroyed almost half of it and greatly damaged the remainder. This year it may be the drouth. We know not.

We are needing rain now—I am trying to get a start in the poultry line but of course our getting here late hindered some and cannot do much this year but hope for better luck another season. We have a splendid cow and she is doing more toward a living than anything else at present. George has put out a small orchard and a number of blackberries and Rasberries and we hope in time to receive some benefit.

I am glad your Children have such good school advantages—I have never felt since we left Le. *[probably Lebanon]* that Earl would ever have the opportunities I so much desired for him as for Louise I do not dare to let myself think of how little the future may hold for her—There is a school house directly across the road from us here—I presume like the majority of country schools they employ a new teacher every year and usually about 15 years behind times.

It is very warm here. Louise and papa are asleep so the house is very quiet. We have no way to go to church this summer so the Sundays will seem long to us. I have often wondered Edith in what part of Le. you reside. I know it must be a great comfort to Mother Flint to have you near her. I think of her so often and how gladly I would remove the clouds that hover over her in so far as we are concerned but I am powerless. You are probably aware that this debt was made before I was a member of your family and for years I supposed it was being canceled. I have often wished I could have a talk with you.

I hope Edith secures the position you spoke of. We have not heard anything farther. I read with pleasure the little papers you sent and most impressed by the poetry written by yourself. Will be glad to hear from the McKendree commencement. I have almost lost track of things and wondered if Victor was to graduate this year.

George has just woke up and is proposing a walk but I think it most too hot however I must quit and get out in the breeze. Don't know when this will get posted we don't get to town only about once a week.

Remember us to Grandma Flint and tell her Louise is the picture of health and (I think) resembles her papa's family very much.

Love to all—Write

Annie

83. Earl Flint to HLT 18 June 1897 [in same envelope as the above]

Dear Hallie,

As mamma was writing today I thought I would write too. Since I have moved out here on the farm I am busy most of the time. I have had to shell about three bushels of seed corn this spring. I have 3 acres of corn just large enough to cultivate which I think will make 50 bushel to the acre. There is a boy named Charley Plain 13 year old living about half a quarter of a mile from here I will have to quit as it is getting dark.

Earl

84. EFT in Toronto to HLT in Lebanon, postcard postmarked 17 July 1897

Toronto, Canada, Sat evening

Dear Children

We have had a very busy day and are too tired to go out tonight. This morning we went *[to]* the M.E. Church rally. I met a girl there from Kokomo who said she knew Prof. Johnsons folks. This afternoon went out to Exhibition Grounds and saw some games and some bicycles races and a fine flag drill. There was an immense crowd. I saw Uncle Wesley. We expect to start home Tuesday A.M. Will write more Monday.

Lovingly,

Mamma

85. EFT in Lebanon to WFT in Carbondale 5 August 1897

Dear boys

Your letter came this morning. We were so glad that you are having a good time. Papa is not very well today, and the younger boys have got the poison on them again especially Harold.

Mr. Goings *[?]* came over yesterday and wanted to know when Victor would be home. He seems very anxious to get off to Piasa. So you must get home as soon as you can.

Now about Mrs. Neary—Mamie was here Tues. She said tell you they missed you very much especially the Thayers. Clemmons brought up five men Monday night. She said tell Will to get home as quick as he can. We have no one to talk dutch to us.

This morning Clemmons came here and said he had a job that he must go to today or lose it and he did not want to lose it and he asked Charlie to go and work until you came. He (Charlie) had just gone to the dentist where he had five teeth taken out and now he is as nervous as an old cat but he thinks he will go. He had just engaged to take care of a horse for someone and the dentist told him to put in all his time [to?] work those wayward teeth into place, so you see he is somewhat busy.

You see you are not gentlemen of very much leisure but you are very much wanted here in this old town. You might have known that the "sun would wobble" if you both went away for so long at a time

Charlie has just come back from the hotel. Mrs. Neary thinks he is too small and we dont know what she is going to do. Poor boy. He lost a job this morning because he was too big and now he loses one because he is too little. I guess that you Willie would better come home on Saturday if you get this letter in time.

Last Monday night G. L. Fish [?] came to make arrangements for coming to school. He has rented the house Prof. Forster used to live in and will rent rooms to students. He left here this morning.

I am afraid you will by some mischance be short of money, so will send you one dollar. You dont have to spend it unless you need it. *[illegible or erased line]* We shall be glad to see you both home again.

Lovingly

Mamma

Love to all the folks.

86. EFT in Lebanon to LWT in Salem "Care S. P. Young" 20 September 1897

Lebanon Ill. Mon A.M.

Dear Lonnie

It is quite cold here this morning. I have been about as usual except perhaps I have coughed a little more. Am taking my medicine all right. The rest are well.

Saturday night Edith received a letter from T. S. Marshall of Salem asking for help in paying Bro. Y. Of course it was my name he saw on the church record but that does not make any difference. I send it to you. Do just as you think we can afford and it will be perfectly satisfactory to me. We will probably not be called upon here but there is an official board meeting at two this afternoon.

There are some letters here for you. I will send them to Mt. Vernon at five this afternoon. We love you and pray for you.

Lovingly

Edith

87. EFT in Lebanon to LWT in Mt. Vernon, "care S. Ill. Conf.," 21 September 1897

Lebanon Ill. Tues. P.M.

Dear Lonnie

Your card was received this morning. A letter came for you this morning forwarded from Vandalia. I send it in this.

Willie is having serious trouble with his foot. You know it has been sore for a week or two and this week it grew much worse. He tried so hard to gather up his laundry yesterday. Henry sent him the horse and buggy or he could not have done it at all. He suffered intensely all night and I could do nothing that helped at all; so today noon we called the doctor in as he was going home. He said the trouble was a bruise on the bone and he froze the heel solid and the[n] lanced it. I am putting hot poultices on every half hour. He is easier and has slept some since dinner.

Bro. P's salary was provided for yesterday. He is donating the last hundred.

Send us what news you can. J. A. Searge seems to be doing well. Bunker Hill has asked for him at a salary of $900. And Bethalto his present work also sends a unanimous call for his return.

Students keep coming in. Goodbye.

Lovingly

Edith

[Laura Lucina Thrall Gould, sister of LWT, died 12 February 1898]

88. EFT in Lebanon to LWT in Bone Gap

Lebanon Mon. 10.15 [Feb. 14, 1898]

Dear Lonnie

Your letter came this A.M. We overslept ourselves and so when Willie got up he went straight to the office & I told him to read what you might write and then send you a card by the morning mail so you could get it tonight.

I was not surprised to hear your news. After a long life of suffering bravely borne she rests. Her life of pain is not the most prominent thought that remains. Her great energy and the amount of work done by her would shame most of the healthy people by whom we are surrounded.

She was a christian and to one of her temperament this meant no idle dream. She was earnest in everything. As I think of her this morning I think of her as a strong character and capable of deep and lasting affections. Those whom she loved so well know this is the uttermost. It is one more tie on the other side. I am so glad Victor went with you. I believe it will be a comfort to the folks for he was always something of a favorite with her.

I hope Carrie will come and you must not fail to persuade her to come and see us whether she can come home with you or come later. I do so want to see her. Mrs. Thatcher came this morning to inquire what was the news and so did Bro. *[illegible]*. How is Solon?

Edith has had so much headache that she did not go out until last night. She is better this morning.

There have come no letters thus far for you but the Dist Adv. is here. Three copies of the paper were placed loose in our box. There were names of subscribers somewhere in the district written on them but no address so I am going to send them back to Bro Tucker. I guess he put them in the Lebanon package by mistake. If any new names should come now I will just let them wait until you come for the paper is out. There is a roll of them here for you.

Give my love to all the folks I would dearly love to have been with you but I could not. I hope to hear from you again tomorrow. I shall think of and pray for you tonight. Edith sends love to all and is going to write to Edith *[Edith Evelyn Gould, daughter of Solon and Laura]*.

Lovingly

Edith

89. EFT in Lebanon to WFT in Vincennes Indiana, 605 Main St., 14 June 1898

Lebanon Ill. June 14. 1898

Dear Willie

Your very welcome letter came a few minutes ago. I think you did fine for your first afternoon and I feel very certain you will do well. I am glad you have company in Mr. Lee. Culver sent for his bill this morning which I shall at once proceed to send him.

Charlie shipped a basket yesterday worth $4.19. Pretty good. He has one new customer for awhile—Ervington. Kate left this A.M. and Jim will go on the same train with this letter. Edie is just fagged out and nearly sick this morning.

We look for Papa home tonight. I must close this or I will miss the mail. I thank you for your newsy letter send us lots [?] such.

Love from All

And especially From Mother.

90. HLT age 12 in Lebanon to WFT in Vincennes, Indiana 20 June 1898

[to Vincennes, IN, 503 Corner Church & 5th St.]

Lebanon Ill. June 20, '98

Dear Will

You are certainly having a good time where you are and I wish that I was with you. Our new neighbor has a very big mouth but it has not got turned this way yet and I hope it wont. She brought her bench and set it out on the side walk and stops most every one who passes to sit down and talk to her. She lives alone.

The new water sprinkler is at work and we have no more dust. In a late letter from you said you going to go swimming and I wish that I could go with you. Docter *[likely a dog]* has gone and not come back yet and so we think he is dead. Charlie and I were in swimming two times today, once at the creek and once at the pond and I wished that we had gone to the pond first and then to the creek to clean off because the water was so dirty.

Edith is going to the convention Thursday morning. We are all well and I hope you are the same.

Lovingly yours Harold

91. EFT in Lebanon to WFT

Lebanon Ill. June 21. 1898

Dear Willie

Your magnificent letter came Monday morning. You dont know how much good it did me. We all enjoyed it. I can assure you I am not going to try to answer it this morning but just send a line with the boys and will answer later. I had a letter from Papa last night and I send one to him today at St. Elmo care C.O. Kimball.

I think Edith will go to Nashville next Thursday morning. Charlie will take her and Phebe Lewis in the buggy to Mascoutah and they will have to start about six in the morning in order to reach the train in time. We send you this morning the last copy of the Leader. I dont think there is much news but still what there is will be home news.

We have just heard from Kate. Two of her directors voted for her and the other went off howling mad and saying "classic words." The contract is not yet signed and she is afraid one of them will weaken. Verily the way of the School teacher is hard. I will write more later.

Lovingly Mamma.

92. EFT in Lebanon to WFT in Vincennes 4 July 1898

Lebanon Ill. July 4. 1898.

Dear Willie

This is the glorious fourth of July but at this date 5.30 everything is so quiet that one would think the glorious fourth had crept into its own pocket, possibly in search of the firecracker it missed yesterday.

There truly was a shameful racket yesterday for Sunday. I was down to see mother and over at the Bishop house there was a constant popping, some time whole bunches sent off at once.

Charlie and Harold are sleeping peacefully. They have made and sold about thirty five cents worth of kites and sold one string of fish for a dime. Then papa gave them a dime so they are not so badly off for patriotic fuel. They have two boxes of colored fire powder and tonight they intend to manufacture and explode red white and blue balls. They have been experimenting for several evenings.

I am about out of paper or I would not use this. It is very cloudy today. I dont know that any of our folks will go away from town today except that Victor will go to O'Fallon this evening. Mother seemed better than usual yesterday. She sent a Lebanon Journal for you with her love. I shall send it out with the Leader. The next three copies of the Van. Dist Adv. *[Vandalia District Advocate]* will be McKendree issues, containing one full page of advertisement of the college and the college authorities will send one thousand extra copies to persons where they think it will do the most good.

Mrs. Charles Cramp a very wealthy woman from the central part of the state will be at Pres. Chamberlains for several days this week. They are hoping for some good results from the visit. I believe she has already given two thousand dollars. Mrs. O Neal's house where the Apostles used to live is fitted up nicely and has summer boarders from the city. They call it McKendree Flats. Aint that sharp?

Edith was writing to you and she just quit to read a letter she had received from Ada Otwell. Bob Otwell has enlisted but will not be likely to pass the examination *[for the Spanish-American War?]* as he is too small.

We, all at the breakfast table this morning, declared that we would rather go to Vincennes to spend the fourth than do anything else. We have heard that there will be a big celebration there with stereoptic attachments. Laying all fun aside we shall be thinking of you boys all day and hoping that you will have a very successful day. If you can conveniently do so please send me a paper with an account of the celebration.

Mr. Bonham who has been sick so long is now sinking and Dr. Waggoner says he can only last a little while.

A letter from Edith Gould that came Saturday brought word that after so long a fight with death Flo. has begun to get better. She is still with Alta. *[Edith Evelyn Gould was the daughter of Solon and Laura Lucina Thrall Gould. Alta was Edith Evelyn's older sister.]* They dont think it best to bring her home for awhile yet. They fear the effect of old association if she should come back before she has recovered a good degree of strength.

We look for Papa home today noon. The district is paying him up much better than usual and this you know is very gratifying.

Well the fourth has crept out of its pocket having found the lost fire cracker and a few more I guess by the increasing racket. I cannot wait to write much more or I shall miss the mail. I hope you have received some more letters by this time.
Did you get a little box with some neckties in it? I sent you one last Thursday or Friday I have forgotten which. Well goodbye Willie dear with hopes for your good success and welfare

Lovingly Mamma

93. EFT in Lebanon to WFT in Vincennes 6 July 1898

Lebanon Ill. July 6, 1898

Dear Willie

I received your letter of Sunday and early Monday morning Monday afternoon. I think you must have hotter weather than we did although Saturday was extremely warm. Sunday afternoon the clouds gathered and about dark it began to rain slowly and continued for two or three hours. Not a great deal of rain fell but it cooled the air and we have had two very pleasant days. I hope they reached out far enough to make you more comfortable.

We thought about you so much on the fourth and wondered how times were with you. We had a rather queer experience on the fourth. Early in the day Faith Watts came over to see if we did not want to go into partnership with them in making ice cream. That suited very well and soon after Mand Watts Bust came to see if we were fixed so we could go over and put our provisions with theirs and have a picnic dinner in their yard. We called the roll at the cupboard door and concluded to join forces. They had a chicken and we had a beef steak. I made some *sataned* eggs (as Victor called them) and Edie mashed some potatoes. I sent

Mand two cans of oysters and she made some oyster salad and also salmon salad.

We had a dish of lemon cake and Mr. Watts bought some sponge cake. After a while he came in and announced to the family that he had invited Pres. Chamberlain's folks and Bro Leoy and his two daughters. Then I saw Prof. Walton coming slowly along the street looking lonely so we invited him and we had a very pleasant crowd. The President asked for your address. I wrote it down and told him you would probably leave there Thursday. He said he would write to you.
Your letter has just come. We are very glad that you made something on the fourth but I feel sorry you are so tired. I thought about you nearly all day and wondered. I dont expect to send you another letter to Vincennes unless you change your plans. Papa is talking of writing to you and so is Victor but we must wait until we hear from you. Mothers folks are well as usual. Goodbye dear.

Lovingly

Mamma

94. EFT in Lebanon to WFT in Washington, Washington County, Indiana 11 July 1898

Lebanon Ill. July 11. 1898.

Dear Willie

Edith received your letter Saturday morning and sent out a card to you by the 8.22. I suppose you have it before now. (Did you ever write with hot ink?) I am writing this out in the summer kitchen with my ink on the outer edge of the range. It is quite cool here. We are going to have fried potatoes and fried bread and oatmeal for breakfast. We are eating very little beef this hot weather except when papa is at home and then he wants it at one meal at the least.

Grandma seems better than she was a while ago. These cool days and nights have helped her. The work on the new church is progressing nicely. We are all going to eat ourselves in[to] apoplexy trying to pay for it. Tonight the Junior Epworth Leaguers are to give an ice cream festival in the parsonage. Next Wednesday night the Epworth League will give (or sell) ice cream on the public square in a few days a hot chicken pie social will be held in the residence of Mrs. Elias. At a later date I can tell you of more spreads.

Last Fri. noon Dr. Waggoner came after Charlie and he has been working there ever since. He and Ray pick the blackberries first thing in the morning beginning at 6 A.M. and then after that they work on a walk he is making. Harold is to collect and send out the laundry today.

Our cypress vines by the old cherry stump have climbed at least fifteen feet and dont seem to have ever dreamed of blooming yet. The leaves are doing well. It is possible that we will have some soon after you get home. I hope you have had fine success in taking orders since you reached Washington Ind. You remember that is the old home place of Miss Laura Wright.

Last week I sent you a copy of the Leader, the Journal and the Dist. Adv. I hope you got them all right. I shall send you the Leader today or tomorrow and a copy of the July Dist. Adv. as soon as it comes out. I will speak to Pres. Chamberlain about your catalogue. They are not yet out. Prof. Walton is in Springfield Ill. overseeing their publication. He went last Thursday morning.

A great wave of enthusiasm in regard the college seems to be spreading over the conference. The Mt. Carmel Dist. Adv. is here now with a full page McKendree advertisement and copious references to the college all through. The Lebanon Dist. will also contain a full page advertisement. John Hearmon, pastor at Mt. Vernon, says *[initials unclear]* Chamberlain is a young Vesuvius. Well I hope that all this flame and smoke will produce some real live coals to warm the altars of Old McKendree this winter and not evaporate in gas.

I do hope you will be able to buy you some new clothes in this order. I know you must need them by now.

Well we have just heard from the mail and did not hear from you. I guess it will come later in the day. Keep up good spirits Willie. We are thinking of you and praying for you here. Come home just when it seems best to you to come. We shall bless the old train that brings you but we dont *[wish]* to be babyish and you understand the circumstances better than we do.

Gid was here Sunday afternoon. I met him at the door and told him that you were not at home. He laughed and came in saying he had had a card from you and it took him half an hour to read it. Well goodbye

Lovingly

Mamma

95. EFT in Belleville to WFT in Washington, Indiana, 18 July 1898

Belleville Ill. July 18, 1898

Dear Willie

I sent to the office last thing before I left Lebanon last Sat. morning hoping to hear from you but got no word. Edith promised to send me any letters that might come from you but there was nothing for me this morning. Edith and I drove over last Saturday A.M. leaving town a little before eight. We brought with us the Epworth Herald, the Union Signal and the Ram's Horn and took turns reading as we drove along. So we had a very pleasant drive. It was not hot and the dust did not bother us until we got very near Belleville.

The folks here are all well. Minnie is in Mt. Vernon attending a wedding. Uncle Wesley will go tomorrow to officiate at the wedding. Aunt Alice Chambers received a summons to Kankakee to take a trial position as attendant in the Hospital for the insane. She left Saturday morning just before we got here. She will stay a month on trial anyway and if the place suits her and she suits the place she will stay.

Annie went back with Edith Sat. and will stay with grandma a while. Uncle Wesley preached a very good sermon yesterday morning and at night the League held a service and a Mr. Sewell Agt. *[agent]* for the Childrens home talked awhile. He expects to place a little boy in a home here.

I shall probably go home next Thursday. We were busy putting up blackberries last week and Edith has some ordered for today. I am anxious to get all we can for they are so nice in the winter. We shall soon have to begin on the pears.

Dont stay out there all summer Will just to say you staid if you are in any danger of falling behind. I shall feel very sorry if you work hard all summer and spend your capital that cost you so much hard work and self denial to accumulate. I have never lost faith in your success in the long run and I want you to know that we are hungry to see you all the time. Of course your experience is worth much to you and contact with the world is worth much but dont pay too heavily for it.

I have thought a great deal about that other company that you are corresponding with. I dont exactly understand what they would expect of you as a general agent next winter and it hardly seems wise to bind yourself for next summer for you dont know just what may turn up.

Now I have another matter to mention to you. You know that Clinton Chamberlain will go to Hutsonville to teach next winter. He wants to give up his laundry agency after his next shipment which will be a week from today. Charlie has been talking to him some about trying to take it up. He offers to sell out for five dollars but papa dont want Charlie to do it and he will probably not say any more to Clinton about it. I dont know if he will make a better offer or not. When they talked about it last he had no other candidate for it. What do you think about trying to capture some of his customers if he leaves no successor? Do you think it would help in the matter if you should write to some of them and explain about Charlie carrying on your work for you this summer, and ask for their patronage. There are all the Chamberlains the Leanders, Duncan, Dr. Fulgham, Charlie Robinson and the Morrises were just trying him last week? Do you think it would be better for you to write to Clint himself?

Now do as you please about the whole matter. I have told you all I know about it. I hope to hear from you tomorrow or Wednesday. I shall say goodbye now. Love you and remember you always.

Your loving Mother

96. EFT in Lebanon to WFT in Flora, Illinois 24 July 1898

Lebanon Ill. July 24. 1898.

Dear Willie

Your last two letters came yesterday and today. Victor was too late for Sunday School this morning and so he compromised matters by going to the mail where he found your last letter. I hope your headache is better before now. I very highly approve of your plan of going down to Bone Gap for a visit. Go and have a good visit. Persuade the folks to let you sleep all you can for a few days. I think you will feel like a new person after that. I think that you will come out clear at the last. Then you will have made your own living and traveling expenses and this is doing very well. I am glad you did not send for money from home. It is not unreasonable that the war views should sell better than others in these exciting times. Will Milton be likely to make much money by the fact that you and Leo [?] swell his profits by 9 cents on each dollar that you collect? I have wondered if he made anything off the goods you ordered in his name. If he didn't he has not made much off of you this summer.

I have not said anything to the President about sending your catalogue to you. You have of late been so much like the little pig who ran about so fast that he could not be counted. Professor Walton says the catalogues are all wrong now because Dr. Fulgham took Miss Ollitie Pesold to Belleville yesterday afternoon and they got married, consequently the assistant prof of music is masquerading under a wrong name. Aunt Gussie said here this morning that she understood that Uncle Wesley had the honor of marrying them. I saw them come in town last night about eight oclock. They drove over in a buggy and as they rode by the M. E. Church a crowd of young toughs who had collected there, headed by Bert Leindly [?], raised a yell and took after the buggy. They tried to raise a racket over them but I dont think they did much.

The church is progressing very nicely. I dont know what Charlie will finally do in regard to the laundry. I wish you would write to him in regard to it. He is better now in fact he is well.

Papa bought himself some very nice glasses about three weeks ago, or less perhaps, and he lost them on the cars last week; then he went to St.

Louis and Dr. Post, the specialist examined his eye for about three hours and then told him that the spot in his eye was in the vitreous humor that he couldn't remove it but that it was likely to remove of itself at any time. He said that he had injured his eyes by wearing imperfect glasses, that he must not wear nose glasses nor glasses that hook over the ears and he helped him to a pair of steel lowed *[?]* glasses that have straight frames. They cost about $2.50. They are different as his eyes are not alike. I hope he will soon be all over it.

Mr. Goings wants you to write to U. T. U. *[?]* and get back that letter of credit that he signed. He says he dont want a paper out with his name attached to it that has $50. on it. I received a long letter from Mrs. Johnson last Thursday. They are doing pretty well.
Yesterday was extremely warm here and so was last night, I dont think today is much improvement. I am glad they sent you our letter. I dont believe this town has been worked for scopes. At least no one has ever called on me since I came here. Shall you call in Salem on your way home? Papa went to Odin to stay all night last Fri. night. He talked a little of going by way of Flora but he would not get there until nearly midnight and would have to leave about four in the morning and so could not hope to see you.

Well I believe I will not write more today. I do so enjoy your letters that I am selfish enough to want one every day. You are climbing one of lifes hills this summer, Willie. There are still higher ones before you but you will never climb another with the inexperience with which you set out last June. You may have lost some faith in humanity but you are now better able to value the world's promises at their real price or worth.

We are hoping to have Myrtle here next year but not certain. Uncle Fletcher *[Flint]* is to have a vacation and he will likely go to Decatur. Gideon Wiggins just went by. Ervington sang in the choir this morning.

Well here I have wandered on for another page. I will surely say goodbye now.

Lovingly

Mamma

97. EFT in Lebanon to WFT, postcard forwarded from Flora to Bone Gap 26 July 1898

Tues. A.M. July 26. 1898

Dear Willie

Your letter to Edith came yesterday. The rain did not reach us until after 5 P.M. Then we had a soaker for about an hour. I am well as usual but never eat anything till noon. We look for Papa sometime today. I thought by the line you wrote in Edith's letter yesterday that you might leave Flora soon so I write again today. It looks like rain again today. Gid is selling Scopes in Trenton. Took twelve orders yesterday. I dont know whether he is going to canvass here or not. Minnie F. is coming out Fri for a visit. Roy will also come. Grandma is well as usual. We hope to hear from you today. I think you keep your accounts with great accuracy. *This is business.* Goodbye.

Lovingly, Mother

98. EFT in Lebanon to LWT 1 October 1898

Lebanon Ill. Oct. 1. 1898.

Dear Lonnie

Your card came this morning and we were glad to hear from you. It has been a very rainy day. Rain began falling before three this morning and continued until nearly noon. The clouds are thick and low and we may have more rain.

Charlie was quite poorly yesterday afternoon and unable to go to Philo last night. I had a hard night, doing no sleeping until after three. Then I slept for several hours not getting up until ten oclock. I have very little appetite. We are taking an extra pint of milk for me to drink hot. I hope to improve now. I cant complain of anything only weakness and restlessness.

Last Monday night when the official meeting adjourned they owed the preacher a little over twelve dollars and the elder twenty seven dollars.

Y. A. Wilson undertook to raise the whole amount and I guess he did. Bro. Leoy told me they are talking under their breath of a new P.E. They say it has been done and can be done again. I will write again Monday and send you some letters.

Lovingly

Edith

99. EFT in Lebanon to LWT 3 October 1898

Lebanon Oct 3 1898

Dear Lonnie

I send in this envelope the mail that has accumulated since you left. I sent a letter to you at Bluford by the five twenty Sat. but sent no mail in it. I was glad to hear from you yesterday. The boys went for the mail if it was Sunday.

Charlie is better but not strong; still he went to school this morning. I am better. Slept better last night than I had for more than a week.

I send this letter out on the noon mail hoping that it will meet you there first thing. I had the union meet at Mrs. Root's for I do not feel strong enough to have them here today.

This letter has in it all the mail that came before ten o clock. I hope you are well.

Lovingly

Edith

100. EFT in Lebanon to LWT 4 October 1898

Lebanon Oct 4, 1898

Dear Lonnie,

I sent you a very full letter yesterday and today I have nothing but a letter from Sherman Young to enclose with this. It came last night. Bro. Leary called a few minutes ago.

I had a very bad night and so feel very weak today. Tomorrow will be my turn for a good day. I have a large bottle of keypophosphites from Fletcher. I think it will last me all the month. It cost me one dollar. Bro. Le. is paid up in full and his traveling expenses also. He told me this morning that he had between twenty and thirty dollars for 1300 Woodley in his care. "We have paid him up in full," he said.

This is a lovely day. I do hope you won't take cold after your wetting. You must sleep as much as you can. I know that will be little enough this busy week.

Charlie is well again. Nearly all the students went to St. Louis today. There are no recitations. Our boys are all at home. Victor rec'd your card this AM.

I hope to hear today.

Lovingly, Edith

101. EFT in Lebanon to LWT 5 October 1898

Lebanon Ill. Oct. 5 1899 *[actually 1898]*

Dear Lonnie

I know you are very busy today but I know you want to hear from home. There is no mail here for you nor has any thing come for the paper.

I have not had any strength to work for the paper as yet. The Dr has begun giving me port wine a teaspoonful every one or two hours. I slept better last night. I do very much wish I knew who would write me a brief sketch of the anniversary of the W. Y. M. S. *[?]* I know you are too busy or I would ask you.

Mrs. Jackson of Metropolis called on me this afternoon. She is here visiting her daughter who is in college. She will go to conference tomorrow but I did not think of it until she was gone. Now if you know of anyone there that you feel free to ask about this all right but if not dont worry over it.

This is a gloomy day. We are all well as usual but me. I think very often of you and hope things will work out all right.
I sent all my other letters by the noon mail but this letter will go out on the five.

Lovingly

Edith

102. EFT in Lebanon to LWT 7 October 1898

[postcard Fri. Oct. 7, 1898]

Dear L.

Your letter this morning is the first we have heard from you since the card you sent Victor from Wayne City so there must be a letter lost. I did not rest well last night, so feel nervous and weak today. Yesterday I was better. Lucile Flint is seriously sick with malarial fever.

I am very much interested in your conference news. Everybody can't be pleased and I think you will arrange things as nearly right as anybody. I understand that J. C. Orr is in town today.

Today is cloudy & we had some rain last night. I hope to hear again from you tonight or tomorrow.

Lovingly E.F.T.

103. ELT (Edith Laura Thrall) in Lebanon to LWT in St. Elmo, Illinois, "Care Rev. D. Shouse" 29 Oct. 1898

Lebanon, Ill Oct 29th, 1898

Dear Papa:

It is now about 4 o'clock in the afternoon. Mamma seems about the same as yesterday at this time. Last night about eight she had a sort of a fainting spell which lasted until after the Dr. came at nine. He stayed an hour or more with her. He left some wine to be given every hour thro' the night.
I stayed with her all night and she rested pretty well—having one nap over two hours long. This afternoon her fever came up again and he sent wine to be given every hour to prevent a return of the sinking spell when the fever leaves her as it did last night. She has slept nearly all the afternoon.

Victor & Willie will stay with her tonight. I think she is getting along as well as we could expect so don't worry at all but pray for us.

Lovingly, Edith.

The Doctor said at noon that Mamma was better. Edith forgot to tell you. Willie.

[Edith Flint Thrall died 10 November 1898 in Lebanon, Illinois]

104. Harold Thrall in Chicago to ?, about November 1908.

. . . It was just ten years since Mama was taken away from us and I tho't what those ten years might have meant to us if God had seen fit to spare her to us; He knows best and I know that she is happy now. If I did not know that it would be a much harder thing for me to understand why she should have been taken away from us so soon. . . .

105. Victor Thrall in Lebanon to sister Edith L. Thrall, 18 February 1908

. . . I have many memories that different places bring to my mind when I am out in town. So often I pass the house where mamma died and many times I live over her last days and long for her. What would it mean for her to visit us here in the parsonage?

The cemetery has filled up far beyond her grave. I like the spot. I think we have a choice lot there. I have been out a number of times. Nine years from the day she left us I buried a Mrs. Whitaker on a lot just east of where we laid Mamma. It was cold and cloudy, within & without…

Index

Index to Flint–Thrall family letters 1870–1898 (+1908) by letter number, not page number. All places are in Illinois unless otherwise noted.

A

Akhurst, 48
Albion, 4
Alcohol issues, 14, 18
Alexander, Bro., 79
Allen, Mrs. Dr., 38
Allyn, Dr., 51
Alma, 22, 73
Altamont, 52
Alton, 36
Amick, Dr., 49
Andrews, Charlie, 63
Anthony, Miss, 13
_____, Mrs., 80
Asbury, Edith, 58
_____, Mrs., 58
Ashley, 19, 21, 23-25, 27

B

Baker, 36
Baker, Bro., 79
_____, Prof., 74
Barnes, Jim, 58
Barr, Prof., 51
Bauchens, Charlie, 58
Beck, Maurie (?), 49
_____, Mrs., 51
Beetler, 17
Belleville, 7, 13, 34, 55, 95, 96
Bennett, Mrs., 34, 40?
Bertha, 18
Bethalto, 87
Bishop house, 92
Blake, May, 81
Bluford, 99

Bogan, Toddy (?), 39
Bone Gap, 4, 26, 28, 58, 88, 96, 97
Bonham, Mr., 92
Bonner, Bro. 25
Borah, Bro., 79
Bowman, Bishop, 72
Boyer, L. J., 81
Bradford, Della, 42, 44, 46
_____, John, 44, 46
Bride, Mr., 1
Briffitt, Sister, 26
Britton, Crete, 72
Brooks brothers, 36
Brown, Carrie, 58
_____, John, 13
Brownlee, Prof., 60
Bryan, 57
_____, "Billy" (William Jennings), 58
_____, Mrs. A. R., 58
Buchanan, "old brother," 38
Bullard, Willie, 58
Bunch, Mrs., 20
Bunker Hill, 87
Bunton, 57
Burkitt, Bro., 79
Burlington (probably Iowa), 7
Burns, 57
Bussong, Peter, 22
Bust, Mand Watts, 93

C

Cady, Olin, 56
Cairo, 34
Calhoun County, 55
Campbell, Charles W., 22, 49
_____, Hannah Caroline, 22, 41, 49, 56, 63
Campbellites, 45, 48
Canada, 52
Carbondale, 21, 25, 30, 85
Carlyle, 34
Carrie (too many to surely identify) 3, 4, 9, 10, 13, 17, 38, 58, 60, 62, 65, 70, 71, 74

Carmi, 17, 23
Carrol, Miss, 56
Carter, Bro., 23
Castle, Mrs., 30
Catterdins, 21
Cavalier, Madam Sorabji, 56
Cellars, Miss, 58
Centralia, 74
Chamberlain, Bro., 71, 74
_____, Clinton, 95
_____, John, 36
_____ (?), Mrs., 49, 76
_____, Pres., 93, 94, 96
Chamberlains, 92
Chambers, Aunt Alice, 95
Chance, Clarence, 58
Chicago, 104
China, 56
Christmas gifts, 19
Cincinnati, Ohio, 4, 49
Cisne, 58
Cistern cave-in, 50
Claflin, 13
Clarence, Missouri, 55
Clemmons, 85
Cleveland, Ohio, 68-70, 72-76, 78, 79
Cline, Sister, 19
Clins, Bro., 6
Clio (singing group), 22, 31, 73
Collins, Dr., 47, 48
Colorado, 7, 49
Columbus, Kansas, 18
Cramp, Mrs. Charles, 92
Cranston, 76
Croquet, 34
Culver, 89
Cumberland Presbyterian Missionary Society, 59

D

Dann, Mrs., 32
Davenport, Mrs., 35
_____, Sister, 79
Deakins, 30
Death, 9
Decatur, 55, 63, 96
Destitute families listed, 58
Dickerman, Bro. Oliver, 27
Dickie, Col., 59
Douthit, Bro., 74
Dreams, 9, 71
Druggists, 18
Duncan, 95
Dunlap, 58

E

Easily (?), Dr., 47
Easterwood (=Eastwood), Mary, 55
Eaton, Y. A., 81
Eau Claire, Wisconsin, 56
Eckert, 51
Effingham, 53, 61
Egypt, 41
Elias, Mrs., 94
Epworth League, 40, 43, 44, 58, 76, 94
Epworth Reading Club, 45
Ervington, 89, 96
Etta, 77
Evans, Mrs., 34, 40
Evanston, 4, 28
Ewing (academy), 26

F

Fager, Prof., 76
Farming, 65, 82
Farmington, Missouri, 19
Farthing, Mamie, 58
Ferguson, Harry, 44

Fifer, Gov. & Mrs., 38
Fikes, Dr., 66
Finley, Dr., 58
Fish, G. L., 85
Fisk, Bro., 81
Flint, Annie E. (Kirkland), 65, 82
_____, Charlie, 60, 63
_____, Earl, 41, 65, 82, 83
_____, Edith Marie, 2-17 (*see also Thrall, Edith Flint*)
_____, Fletcher, 19, 31, 36, 56, 60, 63, 64, 96, 100
_____, George, 7, 41, 60, 65, 82
_____, Gussie, 56
_____, Henry (*see also Flint, Matthew Henry*)
_____, James G., 7, 12(?), 36, 55, 60
_____, John Wesley, 3, 4, 7, 11, 13, 19, 34, 36, 60, 84, 95, 96
_____, Louise, 65, 82
_____, Lucile, 102
_____, Mary [later Nelson], 3, 18, 20, 23, 60
_____, Mary Gedney, 19, 23, 25, 31, 32, 36, 41, 48, 49, 51, 52, 53, 55, 56, 60, 63, 65, 66, 71, 74, 82, 92, 94, 97
_____, Matthew Henry (*see also Flint, Henry*), 7, 18, 19, 33, 38, 55, 60
_____, Minnie, 60
_____, Myrtle, 55 (?)
_____, William, 7, 10, 36
_____, William Winterton, 19, 36, 41, 42, 46, 49, 55-58, 60, 62-65
Flora, 96, 97
Floyd, Mrs., 31
Football, 58
Forbes, Mrs., 56
Forster, Prof., 85
Foster, Bishop, 72
_____, Sadie, 62
Fourth of July 1898, 92
Freeburg, 17
Fulgham, Dr., 95, 96

G

Galbreath, Bro., 79
Gerne, 55
Gid, 97
Gilham, Bro., 68

Housework, 18
Hoyt, 51
Hull, Old Man, 62
Hutsonville, 95
Hypes, E. A., 51
_____, Mrs., 47, 56

I

Ingersoll, Robert, 75

J

Jackson, Mr., 101
Jepson, Genevieve, 36
_____, Prof., 33, 36
Jepsons, 63
Johnson, Mr., 96
_____, Prof., 29, 84
Johnsonville, 56, 58, 81
Johnston, Mrs. Belle, 58
_____, Prof., 70
Jones, Mrs., 38
Junior Epworth League, 94
Junior League, 40, 58, 80

K

Kampsville, 55
Kankakee, 95
Kansas, 18
Kentucky, 57, 81
Kershey, Bro., 13
Ketring, Miss, 52
Kimball, Bro., 61, 66, 67, 79, 81
_____, C.O., 91
Kinmundy, 71, 81
Kinsley (?), 74
Kirk, 51
Kirkham, Etta, 40
Knight, Mattie, 62
Kokomo, Indiana, 84

L

Lake Branch, 6
Laundry agency, 95
Laws, Mrs., 41
Leakin, 57
Leanders, 95
Leary, Bro., 100
Lebanon, Illinois, 1-3, 9, 10, 12, 13, 17, 22, 37, 46, 47, 49, 51, 52, 54, 58, 59, 63, 65, 67-71, 73-78, 80-82, 85-90, 92-103, 105
Le., Bro., 100
Lecavits, 61
Lee, Mr., 89
Leindly, Bert, 96
Leo, 96
Leoy, Bro., 93, 98
Lewis girls, 63
Lewis, Phebe, 91
Little, Bro., 57, 58, 79
_____, Sister, 58
Loar, Bro., 79
Lord, Hattie, 17
Loudens, 55
Louisville, Kentucky 67

M

MacElwain (destitute), 58
MackElwain, Mrs., 58
Mains, Bro., 71
Malarial fever, 102
Marshal, Ella, 35
_____, Harriet, 35, 72
Marshall, Bro., 53
_____, Mrs., 58, 80
_____, T. S., 86
_____, Y. S., 57
Martin, Ben, 35
_____, Gen., 79
_____, Mr., 56
_____, Mrs., 57
_____, Nannie, 43

Roy (Flint??), 97

S

Sager, Mr., 60
Sailor Springs, 57
St. Elmo, 58, 91, 103
St. Jacobs, 74
St. Louis, Missouri, 3, 31, 36, 38, 56, 63, 96, 100
Sale, Bro., 35
Salem, 30, 35, 51-54, 57, 61, 72, 73, 75-77, 79, 80, 86, 96
Samson, 42
Sandoval, 2, 58, 62
Sarge, J. A., 81
Saulsbury, Mrs., 39
Savage, Mrs., 38
Scanthon, Bro., 79
School teaching, 11, 12, 91
Scudder, Dr., 4
Seaman, Jonathan, 48, 74
_____, Mrs. Frank (Jennie), 34, 38, 40, 42, 52, 58
Searge, J. A., 87
Sewell, Mr., Agent, 95
Shay, Mrs., 38
Sheperd, Mrs., 6
Shouse, Rev. D., 103
Shultz, Mrs., 56
Singerfest, 14
Smith, 36
_____, Amanda, 72, 75
Smithboro, 34
Smith (destitute), 58
Soulsby, Mr., 34
Sparkes, Mrs., 38
Spark, S. P., 3
Sparta, 17
Spragg, Mr., 63
Springfield, 38, 56, 62, 94
Squire Farmer's, 66
Stonecipher (?), John, 35
Sullens (destitute), 58
Sunday School Convention, 23

Swahlen, Prof., 8, 17

T

Thatcher, Mrs., 51, 88
Thayers, 85
Thompson, Bro., 57, 58, 74
_____, Fred, 34
_____ girls, 57
_____, Grace, 77
_____, Sister, 35
_____, Mrs., 53
Thompsons, 77
Thrall, Charles H., 25-30, 32, 35, 37, 39, 42, 43, 46, 47, 50, 51, 53, 58, 62, 66, 69, 73, 74, 80-82, 85, 89, 90, 92, 94-96, 98-100
_____, Edith Laura, 17, 19-23, 25-27, 30-34, 37-45, 47, 49-64, 66, 67, 73, 76-78, 86, 88-95, 97, 103, 105
_____, Edith Marie Flint, 17-38, 40-48, 51-63, 65-68, 70-72, 75-77, 79-82, 85-89, 91-104 (*see also Flint, Edith Marie*)
_____, Hannah Caroline, 3, 10, 13, 17 (*see also Campbell, Hannah Caroline*)
_____, Hannah James, 1, 17
_____, Harold "Hallie," 32, 34, 36, 39, 40-43, 45, 47, 53, 58, 62, 63, 65, 73-76, 80, 83-85, 90, 92, 94, 104
_____, Leonidas "Lonny," 1-19, 21-30, 32-38, 42, 44, 45, 47, 52, 54-59, 61, 62, 65-72, 76, 78-81, 85, 86, 88, 89, 91- 93, 96-103
_____, Victor, 19, 21, 22, 25, 26, 28, 30, 32, 37-41, 43, 44, 46, 47, 51, 52, 54, 56- 62, 66- 68, 70-77, 81, 82, 85, 88, 92, 93, 96, 100, 102, 103, 105
_____, William F., 22, 23, 25, 26, 28, 30, 32, 33, 36, 39, 41, 43, 46, 47, 53, 56, 58, 59, 62, 71, 73, 77, 81, 85, 87-97, 103
Toronto, Canada, 85
Trenton, 6, 10, 49, 97
Trigonometry, 3
Tucker, Bro., 88
Typhoid fever, 57, 58

U

Union Temperance Service, 47
Utterback, 35, 57, 58, 62, 75, 77

V

Van Cleve, Bro., 79
Vandalia, 87
Vandeveer, Bro., 79
Vincennes, Indiana, 89, 90, 92, 93

W

Wabash River, 26
Wag(g)oner, Dr., 80, 92, 94
Waggoner, Prof., 49
Walker, 22
Wallar, Bro., 71
Walton, Prof., 93, 94, 96
Warren, Dr., 41
Washington, Indiana, 94, 95
Watts, Faith, 93
_____, Mr., 93
Wayne City, 74, 102
WCTU (Women's Christian Temperance Union), 40, 57
Webster, Grace, 57
_____, Mrs., 57, 59
Weise, Mrs., 38, 42, 43
Wesley, Susannah, 53
West, Bro., 27, 36
Whiskey, 14
Whitaker, Mrs., 105
Whitten, Sister, 35
Wiggins, Gideon, 96
Wilkerson, Bro., 56
Willard, Frances, 57
Wilson, Bro., 79
_____, Rob, 41
_____, Y. A., 98
Window weight noises, 42
Wise, Charlie, 60
Women's Foreign Missionary Society, 66
Women's Missionary Convention, 47
Women's rights, 13, 69, 70
Woodhull, 13